8-7-68

What
Makes
Reagan
Run?

WHAT MAKES REAGAN RUN?

A Political Profile

by Joseph Lewis

McGRAW-HILL BOOK COMPANY
New York   Toronto   London   Sydney

Contents

C705587

Introduction

On November 8, 1966, an event that would have been considered incredible a few years earlier occurred in California. The most populous state in the Union elected as its new governor a middle-aged actor in the sunset of his career who had never served a single day in public office. By nearly 1 million votes, Californians decided they wanted Ronald Reagan to conduct the public affairs of a state whose gross economic output exceeds that of all but six nations in the world. On the night that Ronald Reagan learned that he would become governor, his supporters surprised a nationwide television audience by unfurling a "Reagan for President" banner. As cheers echoed throughout the hall, hardly anyone recalled that Edmund G. "Pat" Brown, the man Reagan had defeated, had won the governorship by a slightly larger margin only eight years earlier. California is consistent only in her inconstancy.

On the California ballot there is a space for each candidate to list his occupation—"attorney," "teacher," "businessman" or "governor." The space below Reagan's name, fittingly enough, was left blank. California had bought a package of unknown contents, a product as carefully marketed and researched as any commodity sold on television. And the techniques which brought Reagan to the State House in Sacramento might some-day deliver him to the White House. A candidate who can excite and entertain California's 8 million voters, as restless and heterogeneous as any electorate, is a hot political property. If you are a winner in California, you can win anywhere.

California is more like the rest of the United States than any other state. What happens in California today often happens in America tomorrow. California has fashioned a way of life that is an exotic metaphor for how most Americans live, feel and dream. With one-tenth of the nation's population, California is a social laboratory for the other forty-nine states and the federal government watching its progress in higher education, mental health, transportation and penology. No other state can match California's geographical, economic and ethnic diversity. Stretching a thousand miles from Oregon to Mexico, California encompasses a land area equivalent to that stretch of Atlantic Seaboard from Cape Cod to Savannah. The flat farmlands in Califor-nia's Great Central Valley look like the Kansas plains; the cotton fields in the San Joaquin Valley like Alabama and Georgia; coastal villages above San Francisco like New England fishing settlements; sage-dotted desert towns like the American Southwest.

Automation, affluence and all the fruits of modern life have blossomed in California, and so have the problems:

political extremism, congested cities, alienation, pollution of natural resources, a wasting of human resources and a growing cynicism about the motives and actions of men in public life.

After decades of unprecedented growth and material abundance, California voted for a change in direction and, in so doing, rejected an activist government that prided itself on tangible good works. Instead, the voters chose a man who promised less, not more. This book tries to explain why California, in the absence of widespread poverty or a major state scandal, voted to change course.

It is no longer possible for politicians to dismiss events in California merely as typical of the social and political aberrations on the continent's westernmost edge. California, which has not spoken forcefully in national affairs up to now, is increasing its social and political leverage, and eventually it may weld a political alliance in the West as identifiable and cohesive as the Old South. The concerns that brought Reagan to power in California are evident throughout the United States, and if California, so generously endowed by Nature, cannot cope with its problems, there is little hope for other states not so abundantly favored.

Because the state is too new and volatile to be self-knowledgeable, it is a vulnerable target for sociologists, and essayists who examine California's hedonistic froth —the casual living, hippies, cults, topless nightclubs and drive-in churches—and remain totally unaware of its reality. The quintessential California, for all its distractions, is a quiet and self-preoccupied place, a kind of national suburban retreat, where Americans flee to escape bad marriages, business failures and crowded cities. Ironically, the amenities that lure Americans to California are threatened by the rush of numbers: more than four-fifths of all Californians live in one-sixteenth of its area. But Americans still migrate to California, and for those who don't the state remains a symbol of a much-desired life style. You can see the California impact in supermarkets, shopping centers, architecture, dress, food and cybernetics.

In some ways, California, energetic, acquisitive and narcissistic, is the best and worst of the American dream, and so is Ronald Reagan. His political rise reflects the growth of a new group in American politics. He appeals to "the forgotten man": California's anonymous millions, neither rich nor poor, who live nine-to-five lives, fight freeways and crabgrass, sweat out thirty-year mortgages and escape to their television sets at night. They are essentially apolitical, and their ranks include well-paid blue-collar workers as well as technicians and Ph.D.'s. They are united in a desire to escape the demands of a complicated and interdependent society. Reaganism appeals to them like the soft, blurry edges of a well-remembered old movie; it is a call to nostalgia and a return to the verities of a generation that believed in itself and the sound dollar. This new class acquired an identity in 1964 when Barry Goldwater crystallized a conservative protest vote. The "forgotten people" transcend conservatism but the arguments of the Right are increasingly appealing to them. They are gaining strength rapidly and, with Reagan as their champion, they could come of age in 1968 or 1972.

Reaganism, a refinement of Goldwaterism, appeals to them because it neither threatens nor challenges; it demands neither sacrifice nor money, and it seeks no new insights. Instead, it reassures the majority of Americans that they possess virtue and truth almost by a divine right of numerical superiority. It is a counterrevolution of the well-fed, well-housed and well-educated against the great social movements of the last three decades. It is capable of mobilizing millions who never cared before about politics, and eventually America must deal with it.

1

The Speech

The 1966 campaign for governor of California began the night of October 27, 1964, when Ronald Reagan electrified a national television audience with a half-hour speech for Barry Goldwater. Until that time Reagan had been an entertainer and professional speechmaker who was known to harbor vague and seemingly unrealizable political ambitions. He had spoken at countless dinners for Eisenhower, Nixon and Goldwater, shaken hands and made small talk at ladies' club luncheons. He had toyed briefly with the idea of running for governor in 1962, but stepped aside when Nixon announced his candidacy. It was apparent that Reagan was thinking about the 1966 race when he made the 1964 Goldwater speech in an obviously hopeless cause.

The speech summarized what he had been saying when he toured the country as a public-relations representative for the General Electric Company. He had worked over the phrases so often, inserting gag lines and removing outdated statistics, that it became known as "The Speech." It was an emotional indictment of the

evils of bureaucracy, pillorying the federal government
for its farm program, urban renewal, taxes, the Tennessee
Valley Authority, foreign aid and welfare.

Four years later, a review of the text in cold print
shows it is overblown and badly in need of judicious
editing. The profusion of statistics—three to a sentence
in some passages—conveys an aura of authenticity although many of his figures are oversimplified, obscure
or irrelevant: "We set out to help 19 war ravaged countries at the end of World War II. We are now helping 107.
We have spent 146 billion dollars. Some of that money
bought a $2-million yacht for Haile Selassie. We bought
dress suits for Greek undertakers. We bought 1,000 TV
sets, with 23-inch screens, for a country where there is
no electricity, and some of our foreign aid funds provided extra wives for Kenya government officials."

By his account, government is not only frivolous and
incompetent, it is an arrogant and self-perpetuating
entity: "Since the beginning of the century our gross
national product has increased by 33 times. In the same
period the cost of federal government has increased 234
times, and while the work force is only 1½ times greater,
federal employees number nine times as many. There
are now 2½ million federal employees. No one knows
what they all do."

In the hands of a less polished speechmaker Reagan's
essential arguments might have sounded like the grous-
ing of a dyspeptic reactionary; but Reagan came across
as reasonable and well-intentioned. He had salted his
indictment with attempts at humor—"A government
agency is the nearest thing to eternal life we'll ever see

on this earth"—and there were flights of lyricism that indicated Reagan not only knew his way around the Right's beloved rhetorical passages, but he could also sway the uncommitted:

> For almost two centuries, we have proved man's capacity for self-government, but today we are told we must choose between a left and right, or, as others suggest, a third alternative, a kind of safe middle ground. I suggest to you there is no left or right, only an up or down. Up to the maximum of individual freedom consistent with law and order, or down to the ant heap of totalitarianism, and regardless of their humanitarian purpose, those who would sacrifice freedom for security have, whether they know it or not, chosen this downward path.

After this lofty beginning, he ticked off the heart of his complaint:

> Already the hour is late, government has laid its hand on health, housing, farming, industry, commerce, education, and to an ever increasing degree interferes with the people's right to know.

When the Goldwater campaign managers first read the speech they went up in flames. Goldwater's chief consultants, Denison Kitchel and William Baroody, wanted to substitute a tape of a low-key "Brunch with Barry" because they felt the Reagan speech was too negative and querulous. There were also complaints that Reagan was promoting his own dream of inheriting the conservative movement without regard for Goldwater's Presidential candidacy. The senator had been grievously hurt by his own statements about Social Security, and his advisers worried about a paragraph which speculated as to whether the system could be made voluntary.

The subsequent fight over use of the Reagan speech exposed a factional division among California's conservatives, among whom, in 1964, was former Assemblyman Joseph Shell, a leading choice for governor. Many conservatives resented Reagan as a glib newcomer who, without having served a day in the ranks, was using the Goldwater candidacy to get a head start for 1966. The Shell supporters knew that a thirty-minute talk on national TV would give Reagan an incalculable advantage in California. While the argument raged, Goldwater's television committee refused to release funds for the telecast unless the speech was allowed. A group of wealthy California conservatives argued in Reagan's behalf that they were tired of losing elections and wanted a winner at all costs. If this actor, who had once been a liberal Democrat, could charge the voters' imagination, then he was their choice. Reagan himself assured Goldwater, "There isn't one kooky thing in the speech—it's the same one I have been giving up and down the country for years." Finally Goldwater consented, convinced that the speech could not hurt him any more than his own statements.

If another Republican had made that speech it would

have been a dud. But those who objected to its tone reckoned without the impact of Ronald Reagan. Furthermore, the speech came at precisely the right moment, shoring up Goldwaterites who had dreamed of a hidden conservative vote that would emerge in 1964. It hadn't. But the impeccably dressed man with the well-modulated voice held out a vestige of hope for 1966 and beyond. Conservatives who saw Reagan on TV saw the possibility of a new leader who would avoid Goldwater's pitfalls.

Moderates and independents who shied away from zealots were quietly impressed by Reagan's air of reasonableness (which was somewhat at odds with what he was saying). To his audience, the speech was fresh and incisive; the audience did not know it was a rehash of set phrases and anecdotes that he had been delivering for years. California's politicians were impressed, too. The questions raised by Reagan's speech did not matter any more than the points John F. Kennedy made in his historic TV debates with Nixon. What counted was that Reagan had the ability to come through loud and clear on television, to register with a distracted and dispirited public. His air of restrained indignation matched the audience's mood in 1964. He delivered his speech as though he were saying it for the first time. Part pedagogue, part pitchman, Reagan salted the talk with enough information, culled from *The Reader's Digest* and *Congressional Record*, to gloss over his sweeping accusations with a mantle of factuality. Paragraph by paragraph, he soared to a bravura finale that sounded like Jimmy Stewart's oration in *Mr. Smith Goes to Washington:*

... We are faced with the most evil enemy mankind has known in his long climb from the swamp to the stars. There can be no security anywhere in the free world if there is not fiscal and economic stability within the United States. Those who ask us to trade our freedom for the soup kitchen of the welfare state are architects of a policy of accommodation. They tell us that by avoiding a direct confrontation with the enemy he will learn to love us and give up his evil ways. All who oppose this idea are blanket indicted as warmongers. Well let us set one thing straight: there is no argument with regard to peace and war. It is cheap demagoguery to suggest that anyone would want to send other people's sons to war. The only argument is with regard to the best way to avoid war. There is only one sure way—surrender ...

... Should Moses have told the children of Israel to live in slavery rather than dare the wilderness? Should Christ have refused the Cross? Should the patriots at Concord Bridge have refused to fire the shot heard round the world? Are we to believe that all the martyrs of history died in vain?

... You and I have a rendezvous with destiny. We can preserve for our children this the last best hope of man on earth or we can sentence them to take the first step into a thousand years of darkness. If we fail, at least let our children and our children's children say of us, we justified our brief moment here. We did all that could be done.

As expected, the speech did nothing for Goldwater, but it made Reagan politically. The campaign headquarters staggered under a deluge of contributions, telephone calls and congratulatory wires. The reaction to the speech was so wild that the Goldwater committee reshowed it a dozen times; private citizens who had never participated before in politics sent checks and money orders with instructions that the funds be used to help get Reagan additional exposure. More than a half-million dollars in contributions poured into headquarters in the campaign's last days, helping to pull the Goldwater organization out of the red.

For years the American Right had hungered for a national spokesman with political sex appeal. Goldwater was too blunt and abrasive for all but a committed few. But when thousands of people watched Reagan saying essentially the same things, the message was much more palatable. His manner was friendly and engaging, devoid of the bitterness that often crept into conservative speeches. He looked sophisticated and urbane, even though his message was corny and parochial; he exuded sincerity and avoided excessive zealotry.

In 1952, when Reagan was still a Democrat, the late Senator Robert Taft of Ohio had spoken with force and conviction for conservatism, but his Midwestern twang and American Gothic features were doomed in a personality contest with a glittering war hero, Dwight D. Eisenhower. Now, in the dying days of the Goldwater campaign, the American public got a preview of post-Goldwater conservatism: Reagan combined Taftian beliefs with Ike's charm.

The rough spots in the text—phrases like "ant heap of totalitarianism" and questions about Social Security—were submerged in the overwhelming acceptance of the Reagan image. Here was no stuffy, starched-collar type with pince-nez and watch fob protruding from vest pocket, but an informal, ageless executive personality equally at ease at a board meeting or a coffee klatsch.

The reaction to the speech convinced wealthy Goldwater backers in California that Reagan was their man. As congratulations poured in, three influential California conservatives—Henry Salvatori, an industrialist; Holmes Tuttle, a Los Angeles auto dealer; and the late A. C. Rubel, head of Union Oil Company and a leader in the ill-fated California right-to-work campaign of 1958—decided to form a fund-raising group, "Friends of Ronald Reagan."

And so began one of the fastest build-ups in American political history, for a man still suspect to many conservatives who remembered him as a onetime liberal and who felt an aversion to actors in politics. His conversion from liberalism had left Reagan defensive, and in recent years he had made many embattled statements to demonstrate his conservative credentials. At a Goldwater dinner in Los Angeles' Biltmore Hotel, for instance, Reagan shucked off the façade of amiability and evoked instant anger. "There's a conspiracy in the Eastern liberal press," he told an audience of Western, Right-thinking Americans, "and we know what *they* are up to. *They* are trying to discredit a great American by creating a false image and running against that. But *they* aren't going to get away with it." It was standard Goldwater cant, but Reagan delivered it as though he had discovered a new insight: there were plotters and he was exposing them. An angry roar of approval rose from the crowd; Reagan got more applause than Goldwater, who breezed through his speech.

It was clear that Reagan had the capacity to set the Right on fire with his righteous indignation, but his fiery utterances of 1964 would have to be toned down if he hoped to get broad support. His backers considered his previous dragon-slaying speeches the temporary aberration of a man who wanted at all costs to win acceptance in the conservative camp.

Salvatori, Tuttle and Rubel were convinced that Reagan's excesses were behind him and that he could campaign as a "no labels" Republican who transcended factional lines. The television address ended all doubts. "When I saw Ronnie on television," said Henry Salvatori, the chief Reagan backer, "I knew he was our boy!" Salvatori, who exerted heavy influence in the Reagan campaign, has been a remote but important figure in California politics for more than two decades. Most of the time, Henry Salvatori has been content to stay in the background while lesser figures have jumped in and out of the headlines. A skilled fund-raiser, he has dabbled in a number of rightist projects in Southern California. For instance, he once formed an organization dubbed "The Anti-Communist Voters League," which rated candidates on their anti-Communist quotient. (One candidate who flunked the "test" was Houston Flournoy, a moderate Republican, who was elected State Controller in 1966.)

Salvatori steadfastly denies that he is an ultraconservative, and he insists that his militant anticommunism is simply good Americanism. In his fight against communism Salvatori has contributed heavily to various causes, including $300,000 for a school of anti-Communist research at the University of Southern California and $1 million for a study of individual liberty at Whittier University.

Salvatori is a silver-haired man with a profile that looks like an engraving on an old Roman coin. He was born in Italy and came to the United States at the age of four. His father was a wholesale grocer in Philadelphia, and Salvatori studied electrical engineering at the University of Pennsylvania and received an M.A. in physics at Columbia. After further study at the University of Oklahoma and California Institute of Technology, he formed his own oil exploration company in the Thirties and later acquired an oil-drilling firm.

Until he discovered Reagan, Salvatori had been virtually unknown to the voters, but his is a potent voice in the GOP's inner circle. He was one of 200 wealthy Californians who contributed to the private fund for Richard Nixon which almost cost Nixon the Vice-Presidential spot on the ticket in 1952. It was after the press exposed the fund's existence that Nixon made his "Checkers" speech on national TV, and convinced the public that the contributions were legitimate and that he had not enriched himself.

Ten years later Salvatori tried to reconcile angry conservatives to the gubernatorial candidacy of Richard Nixon. He invited Nixon and his defeated primary rival,

Joe Shell, to his Bel-Air mansion and exacted a grudging
promise of support from Shell. But many of Shell's supporters sat on their hands because of Nixon's repudia-
tion of the John Birch Society, and, partially as a result
of their disinterest, Pat Brown won reelection and a
short-lived reputation as a giant-killer.

Both Reagan and Salvatori have been coy in describing their relationship. During the 1966 campaign
Reagan's staff took great pains to say that Salvatori had
not been seen at campaign headquarters in weeks although, by an irony of coincidence, Salvatori and
Reagan were meeting at that moment in the campaign
office. The two men visited each other in the privacy of
their homes to plan the tactics of 1966 and beyond. After
Reagan was elected, the Los Angeles *Times* printed in
its Sunday magazine, *West*, an innocuous article about
the ten most prominent men behind the new governor.
Salvatori was included in the list, and an assistant to the
governor said that Reagan was displeased. "It reinforces
the charge that Ron is a glamorous mouthpiece for special interests."

In his rare public statements Salvatori emphasizes
that he has no hold on Ronald Reagan. "We're friends,"
he carefully explains. "I supported him, and Ron re-
spects my opinions."

This bland appraisal of their relationship is belied by
Salvatori's efforts to get the Presidential nomination for
his friend. He has close contacts with oil interests in the
Southwest which contributed heavily to the Goldwater
campaign, and Reagan is popular with the same interests. Salvatori and other California conservatives are

convinced that they have a potential big winner for the first time in years, and they have been trying to play down their association with the Right. "I am for the graduated income tax," says Salvatori. "I have never accused the State Department of treason. I *have* said the State Department has unwittingly followed the Communist line, but I have never accused it of treason; only the extremists do that."

Although Ronald Reagan does not meet the purist's qualifications for a candidate on the Right, knowledgeable conservatives like Salvatori realize that Reagan is as close to their thinking as any major Presidential candidate is likely to get. The results of 1964 convinced them that a new face like Reagan could win by merging the Goldwater constituency with a pivotal bloc of dissatisfied Democrats and independents. Thus the Goldwater campaign provided a valuable primer for the political education of Ronald Reagan.

2

A Triumph of
Type-casting

*You know, sometimes at home with Nancy, I kinda
complain a little bit because in recent years, due to my
Guild experience, and all the experience in those other
things—you know Hollywood has a way of type-casting
you—I had a feeling that my career theatrically was suf-
fering because Hollywood wasn't looking at me as an
actor.*

*Now, to turn around and find that suddenly now that
I want to be something else besides an actor—everybody is saying that I'm an actor. I'll tell you, I'll probably be the only fellow who will get an Oscar post-
humously.*

Ronald Reagan, press conference,
March 30, 1966, Orange County, California

Although he has rebelled all his life against type-
casting, Ronald Wilson Reagan is a triumph, not a victim, of it. His strength is his shining image as the earnest,

13

pleasantly naïve "citizen politician," a role of dewy-eyed ingenuousness which he plays exquisitely, having prepared for it in fifty films. Ironically, Ronald Reagan was never a natural actor; he lacked the soaring imagination, the esthetic fire, to be a first-rank professional. But he is a master politician who senses where the power lies and acts accordingly.

As an actor he was afflicted by an All-American image that Hollywood regarded as a lack of sex appeal; as a would-be politician, he had to wait until Senator George Murphy made it before he could get serious backing. Before 1964 a Reagan candidacy would have been considered a joke. But Reagan, who was serious about his political ambitions long before anyone else was, now has sex appeal to burn—because those apple-pie qualities that bore movie fans reassure voters—and today he is the hottest property in politics. He flourishes precisely because he appears to be what he is not: an amateur. While others suffer under the burden of being "professional politicians," Ronald Reagan is adroit enough to mask his stagecraft, and so he retains his amateur standing.

It is typical of Reagan that he is misunderstood by friends as well as by critics. Despite his simplistic oratory and apparently seamless surface, even long-time acquaintances concede that he is not an easy man to understand. The most telling insights into Reagan's character are derived from his autobiography, *Where's the Rest of Me?* (Duell, Sloan and Pearce, 1965), written with Richard G. Hubler, an English instructor at San Fernando Valley State College and a onetime journalist and movie writer. A conservative admirer, editor-columnist William F. Buckley, sized up the autobiography: "It *is* an unfortunate book, not at all for what it says, which is wholesome and intelligent, but for the way it is said. There is no doubting that it is primarily responsible for the insiders' assumption that the governor is a hopeless cornball." Buckley makes the point that Reagan should not be held responsible for the book's essentially pedestrian approach and that he is somehow the victim of another man's style. Nonetheless, Reagan, who prides himself on having written his 1966 campaign speeches, has a recognizable style, and it is evident throughout the book. He also approved every line and paragraph of the aptly titled autobiography, which actually reveals more than it intends to.

The prose is ponderous and self-conscious. He begins on the first page with his birth: "My face was blue from screaming, my bottom was red from whacking, and my father claimed afterward that he was white when he said shakily, 'For such a little bit of a fat Dutchman, he makes a hell of a lot of noise, doesn't he?'

". . . As for myself, ever since my birth my nickname has been 'Dutch' and I have been particularly fond of the colors that were exhibited—red, white and blue . . ."

Describing his childhood, Reagan declares: "My existence turned into one of those rare Huck Finn—Tom Sawyer idylls. There were woods and mysteries, life and death among the small creatures, hunting and fishing; those were the days when I learned the real riches of rags."

What emerges from the pages is a complex and ambitious man who, because of conditioning and the pervasive influence of Hollywood, cultivates a façade of relaxed ingenuousness. The subliminal message of the autobiography, confirmed by the testimony of colleagues and schoolmates, reveals an essentially cautious man, endowed with a retentive memory and a quick grasp of essential facts, who tries to calculate and program every step in his professional ascent. The book reveals a man who worked hard to rise from humble beginnings and who apparently believes he did it largely on his own. There is nothing in his writing that indicates concern with others who cannot do the same.

Reporters who covered his 1966 campaign and his activities as governor have glimpsed a multi-layered psyche. There is Reagan the salesman: friendly, energetic and brimming with statistics and campaign anecdotes; then there is a brooding loner who rebels against the demands made on the public Reagan. The second Reagan, who emerges in private audiences with politicians and reporters, does not suffer fools gladly; he is stiff with strangers and feels frustrated by unsympathetic listeners. When I first met Ronald Reagan, for a brief interview early in the 1966 campaign, I saw both Reagans. Smiling and relaxed at first, he repeated set pieces that he had been using for years and, when that failed to go unchallenged, he became increasingly distant. He used up much of the allotted time with unresponsive answers to unwelcome questions, relying largely on huge chunks of his Basic Speech. When it became apparent that his visitor wanted more than he was willing to give, he froze into glacial hostility. He stared wordlessly at his listener, shifted in his seat and then arose to announce that "another delegation is waiting for me." It was, precisely to the minute, the end of the half-hour he agreed to give me. I left with the impression that, far from being the patsy the Democrats portrayed in 1966, he was a steely, stubborn, somewhat defensive man who is convinced that anyone who is not avowedly sympathetic is an enemy.

When George Murphy campaigned in 1964, he plunged into the ritual nonsense with a Happy Warrior fatalism, brimming with blarney, buttonholing strangers in supermarkets and eagerly challenging hecklers. But Reagan is more thin-skinned and becomes defensive when he senses disagreement; his lips compress into a tight and wary smile until he knows the audience is sympathetic. Instinctively, he recoils from intimacy, while Murphy the campaigner encourages it. When both were active in the Screen Actors Guild in the Forties and Fifties, George Murphy was a Republican and Reagan a liberal Democrat. When Murphy warned about Communist infiltration into the movie industry, Reagan dismissed him as an "arch reactionary." Now the two men have a correct, if not close, relationship. When Murphy campaigned in 1964 he occasionally ran into Reagan, who was making speeches for Goldwater.

When the two met on the campaign trail they greeted each other perfunctorily and each hurried about his business. Differences in their personal chemistry precluded rapport; besides, Murphy was trying to avoid the Goldwater label.

In their efforts to topple Reagan the Democrats made

the mistake of believing their own mythology. They dismissed him as an opportunist—a shallow and insensitive one, at that. But if he is an opportunist, he also epitomizes the values of a political system which produces Nixons, Kennedys, Romneys and Percys. In politics, opportunism is the name of the game, and Reagan differs from the herd because he is so skillful at playing the game while pretending not to. (Actually, the term opportunist has no relevancy in politics: you play the game or you are out.) If Reagan is an opportunist, so is every successful politician. When he was a left-wing liberal he worked hard at it, speaking out for controversial causes and unpopular politicians, and as a right-winger he did the same. Today Reagan is still in transit, trying to carve out his own identity, but torn between an inborn caution and a gambler's instinct to grab fate by the forelock.

"When Ronnie was a liberal," recalls Paul Ziffren, a liberal Democrat and former national committeeman, "he had the guts to appear on the same platform with Helen Gahagan Douglas [who was excoriated as "The Pink Lady" and defeated by Nixon in 1950 in one of California's roughest campaigns], and I remember that Pat Brown was too scared to acknowledge her presence on the ticket."

While Reagan took great pains to work out his own speeches, the Democrats characterized him as an amiable lightweight who excelled only at mouthing someone else's lines. Ironically, Reagan is at his worst when he reads from a *prepared* text, possibly because of his nearsightedness; as a speechmaker, he excels when he wings it without a text.

His critics also contend that he got into politics because his career declined. But politics has always been his first love; acting is what Reagan did for a living. He was more involved with politics, community problems and the Screen Actors Guild than he was with the asinine, one-dimensional scripts he usually got. Although he was never a superstar, he made a lot of money in movies and television and, despite ups and downs in a highly competitive business, he survived longer than most. He started going downhill in the movies because he could not make the transition from ingenue to mature performer, but he got a second wind as a television personality.

It is no secret in Hollywood that he had political ambitions for years, but the cosmopolitans of the movie industry never considered him more than an overgrown Boy Scout, an earnest provincial who was constantly crusading for something or other. When he became a candidate Hollywood blossomed with bad jokes: "Lights, cameras, legislation!" "No retakes in the governor's mansion." And the oldest gag of all: Jack Warner (who was one of Reagan's earliest supporters) declares: "Ronnie for governor? No. Jimmy Stewart for governor. Ronnie for best friend." Even the nickname, Ronnie, seemed calculated to diminish his stature, and his air of clean-cut sincerity led to other sobriquets: Mr. Clean, Captain Nice, Mr. Wonderful. Ronnie had always been a big laugh-provoker, chiefly because he was considered too corny to be true.

Hollywood's sophisticates considered him a well-meaning bore with intellectual pretensions, a man who read *The Reader's Digest* and quoted from it. He was too impassioned for the languid life-style of the movies and he loved to talk even when his audience responded with glazed eyes. "You ask Ronnie what time it is," an actress complained, "and you get an hour's lecture on how to make a watch." It is easy to discount, but hard to dislike, a man who sticks, come hell or high water, to quixotic positions: he lectured everyone about the inequities of the progressive income tax and he speculated in earnest that the military might have ended World War II a lot sooner if they had used horse cavalry. Far from being embarrassed when challenged, Ronnie redoubled his arguments and usually overwhelmed his listeners with a profusion of obscure statistics.

Hollywood saw the naïve side of his nature, the embattled provincial sticking by his guns in the midst of towering yawns. He made the cocktail party liberals uncomfortable because he cared terribly about the opinions of others, especially the achievers, and yet he wanted to be accepted on his own terms. Perhaps Hollywood felt that Reagan's pursuit of his own private dreams was a bit too naked, too self-intoxicated; it took many years for Reagan to develop a protective shell.

Like many Californians, Reagan came from the Midwest, and his early years with few exceptions comprise the pure Americana that campaign managers dream about. He was born February 6, 1911, in Tampico, Illinois, to John Edward and Nelle Clyde Reagan, one of two sons. (His brother Neil, who is two years older, now is a vice-president with the McCann-Erickson Advertising Agency in Los Angeles.) The Reagans lived in rented homes in a succession of small towns in downstate Illinois: Galesburg, Monmouth, Dixon and Tampico. Throughout his childhood Reagan knew the shabby, frayed edge of lower-middle-class respectability and of families whose lives are clouded by economic anxiety.

His father, Jack, was an Irish Catholic and an outspoken liberal Democrat who went against the grain of the Midwest's small-town ethos: conservative, Republican and Protestant. Jack Reagan never made more than $55 a week in "the shoe business," in which he worked most of his life as a salesman, clerk and erstwhile partner in a shoe store. Jack had a passion for liquor, people and politics; he was a rollicking extrovert who could tell a good story and make people like him even when they felt they should disapprove. He also had a deep sense of social responsibility, which caused him to walk out angrily from a hotel that would not admit Jews. And once he forbade his sons to see the film *Birth of a Nation*, because it glorified the Ku Klux Klan. Although he was poor and, by the stuffy standards of small towns, slightly disreputable, Jack was a proud man, whose vision could never square with the dreary reality of living on the edge of poverty. Ronald Reagan, alternately pained by his father's excesses and proud of his individualism, learned to go to his mother for counsel. It was Nelle Clyde Reagan, a Scots-English Protestant, who put the Reagan boys on the path of conventional righteousness. She saw that they attended Sunday services at the Christian Church, taught them to read before they started school, and impressed on them the value of hard work and piety. All his life, Ronald Reagan has been torn by twin influences: Jack and Nelle Reagan. He was the kind of boy his mother wanted, friendly, dedicated and courteous, and yet there was another side, that of the dark and impulsive dreamer, that Reagan apparently repressed for years.

In his autobiography Reagan describes a boyhood that, aside from his father's problems, sounds like a scenario from an Andy Hardy movie. He was the neighborhood paragon: a dedicated if not brilliant student, a hard worker and an enthusiastic joiner. He was a sensitive and serious boy whose hair fell over his spectacles; skinny and nearsighted, he seemed all elbows and Adam's apple. As a freshman at Dixon High School he stood only 5 feet 3 inches and weighed a mere 106 pounds, but he threw himself into games and school projects. He played football and acted in school plays. He was involved in all of the campus activities, and in his senior year was elected president of the student body. He was, in sum, the kind of boy our mothers tell us to admire but whom we secretly dislike and envy, without being able to say why. He was almost too good to be true, as if he had swallowed the American Dream whole and was trying to live every page of an Horatio Alger story.

He conformed to all the hallowed rules, and, if he had any doubts, he submerged them in activities and good works. He rarely did anything for the sheer aimless hell of it, and his unyielding determination to escape his

father's economic frustration drained him of the sponta-
neity and exuberance that are every child's birthright.

Young Reagan believed that college was the ticket
out of his parents' marginal existence. And, to earn
money for college, he dug cement foundations and
worked as a lifeguard during the summer, saving his
money faithfully.

Eureka College, a gemlike campus with ivy-shrouded
Gothic towers, was Ron's goal. Eureka was a coed institution, supported by the Christian Church, and it had an
enrollment of less than 250 students. Young Reagan, who
had shot up to 6 feet in his senior year in high school, got
an athletic scholarship that paid half his $180 tuition and
guaranteed him a job. He raked lawns, washed dishes
and waited on tables to meet his college expenses, and
the financial strain grew so intense that he almost quit
after his freshman year. But he stayed on, partly because
he wanted to be near his high-school sweetheart, Mar-
garet Cleaver, partly because no opportunities awaited
him in the workaday world back home. It is easy, in the
light of his college hardships, to understand why Governor Reagan now is so unsympathetic to the concept of
free higher education in California. He worked like a
slave to get through four years of college, and in the
permissive, affluent atmosphere of the University of
California, he sees upper-middle-class children, whose
hands have never been soiled by work, rebel against the
very goals that Reagan worked so hard to achieve.

In Reagan's freshman year, 1928, he had his first confrontation with the academic bureaucracy—but from

the other side of the issues. He joined a student protest against an austere and rigid college administration, whose puritanical social policies angered the student body. Eureka operated under a strict moral code that prohibited smoking and drinking. Dr. Bert Wilson, president of Eureka, occasionally lectured the students about ballroom dancing, which he regarded as the Devil's pastime. The students nursed their grievances and waited for a chance to attack the fundamentalist college president. When Dr. Wilson eliminated a number of courses for economic reasons, the students seized on the academic cutbacks as a cause and organized a boycott of classes that lasted a week. Meanwhile they held meetings and called for the president's resignation. Reagan, who loved to declaim even as a seventeen-year-old freshman, was summoned to make a speech, and he responded with an impassioned oration that left the students cheering and stamping. Although he has forgotten the words, Reagan recalls, "I discovered that night that an audience has a feel to it, and, in the parlance of the theater, that audience and I were together." Classmates at Eureka recall that Reagan participated in, but did not lead, the student revolt; he was always the speechmaker, "Paul Revere sounding the alarm," as he put it. After a series of maneuvers the students won their battle and Dr. Wilson resigned. More than thirty years later Governor Reagan warned protesting students at the University of California, "Obey the rules or get out."

On campus Reagan became an all-out striver, who was determined to go the full college route. He joined the right fraternity, Tau Kappa Epsilon, worked as a reporter on the student paper, *The Pegasus,* served as feature editor of the yearbook, joined the freshman debate team, served as cheerleader during basketball season, was elected president of the student senate and the Booster Club and acted in campus plays. His nearsightedness kept him out of baseball and basketball, but he could play football. He sulked on the bench most of his first year. "I told everyone who would listen that the coach didn't like me," Reagan relates. "I was the victim of unreasoning prejudice. I needed a damn good kick in the keister, but how can you kick something that's permanently planted on a bench?" But he perked up after he made first string as a 175-pound guard. Schoolmates remember him as an ordinary player with considerable desire.

Reagan graduated from Eureka in 1932, with a bachelor's degree in sociology and economics. His classmates had kidded him about his dramatic ambitions, which were evident at Eureka. Reagan replied, "If I'm not making five thousand a year when I'm five years out of college, I'll consider these four years here wasted." Five thousand dollars was a considerable sum in 1932 but, as Reagan recalls, he made good on that boast in exactly five years. Although he wanted to be a movie star, he was shrewd enough to realize that no one with sense assaults Hollywood directly. So he took a series of temporary jobs, always calculating and shaping his career so he could be ready for the next advance. Eventually, Radio Station WHO in Des Moines, Iowa, hired him as a sportscaster to broadcast Big Ten and Notre Dame football games and to re-create major-league baseball games.

In those days sports announcers outside the major-league cities often re-created games from cryptic Western Union messages. It took a genuine gift of gab and a lively imagination to fashion a full-fleshed baseball game from the bare-bones inning-by-inning summaries on the telegraph wire, a challenge which helped Reagan develop. his natural speechmaking gifts for hyperbole and melodrama. Broadcast re-creation of baseball games is a dying art, and there are few who can master it. But Reagan was superb at it. Because of television, hardly anyone notices one of his most potent assets—his voice, which he developed as a broadcaster.

Reagan's voice is like musical scoring in a film; when it is really good, it is not noticed. As familiar and soothing as breakfast coffee, it conveys warmth, knowledge-ability, confidence and authority. It neither grates on the nerves nor lulls the listener to sleep. Richly timbred and carefully filtered, it has the regionless accents of an impersonal but benevolent announcer. There is no questioning its authenticity, whether it is making foreign policy pronouncements or ticking off scores of the hometown team. A virile, warm voice like Reagan's can be professionally refined but it cannot materialize from nothing. It is a gift from Heaven, a priceless asset for a chief executive trying to reassure the lonely millions who are bewildered by an urbanized and restless society. It is a voice seemingly free of artifice or regionalism; no hint of slang, drawl or twang, nothing of the slicker or of the huckster. Yet it can arouse, inspire and sell anything. It is as American as the flag, and it goes beautifully with the image.

Even as a sportscaster in Des Moines, Reagan kept his eye on bigger things. When the Chicago Cubs left for spring training at Catalina Island, off the Los Angeles coastline, Reagan persuaded the station to let him accompany the team. The year is 1937, and Robert Taylor, Errol Flynn and Clark Gable are the big stars in Hollywood. When he gets to the big city, Reagan looks up a friend, Joy Hodges, who once worked as a vocalist for the Des Moines station. At dinner he asks her to help him get a screen test. This request was not so improbable in the Thirties; in that era Hollywood was the movie capital of the world, and it needed a constant supply of talent for hundreds of films produced each year, including the B films required to fill the insatiable demand for double features. The B's were usually remakes of the expensive A movies, and they were filmed on the run with obscure names and little regard for production values, with the subject matter running heavily to melodrama, Westerns and the now defunct women's tear-jerkers.

Joy Hodges introduced him to an agent, who sized up the broad-shouldered, twenty-six-year-old former athlete and, proclaiming that he had found "another Robert Taylor," arranged an audition at Warner Brothers. There is only one additional, and exceedingly brief, reference to Miss Hodges in Reagan's autobiography. She is one of the book's many supporting players who apparently exist only to give Ronald Reagan a leg up and, having done so, return to the shadows. There is no indication in the book that he has done similar favors for anyone.

Reagan learned immediately that Hollywood was

most interested in those who could not care less about working in show business. So he made it clear that he could not wait too long for the results of his screen test. In a few days his agent received a wired offer of a $200-a-week contract. Reagan became an actor, and in the first years of his new career appeared in a staggering number of B films, almost all of them gross, sentimental and cynically made. "I became the Errol Flynn of the B's," Reagan recounts. "I was as brave as Errol, but in a low-budget fashion." But there was a difference: Errol Flynn invariably got the girl. In his roles, Reagan usually was cast as the ineffective nice guy, the archetypal square who does everything by the book and is rewarded with the knowledge that the other guy, usually a devil-may-care scamp like Errol Flynn, gets the leading lady.

The titles of his films tell the story: *Love Is on the Air* (his first, a sixty-one-minute epic), *Girls' Night Out, Bedtime for Bonzo, Swing Your Lady, Hollywood Hotel, Boy Meets Girl* and on and on until he is fixed indelibly in the celluloid mills. He is cast as an American Candide, asexual, deferential and naïve, and in some ways his public image seems like an amalgam of all the lighter-than-air, simplistic characters he was required to portray.

Gradually he got better parts, in A films. He played George Gipp, the talented and eccentric halfback at Notre Dame in *Knute Rockne, All American*. Reagan happened to have his old college football pictures in his apartment and he brought them along to convince a skeptical producer that he was right for the part. In the film he runs 80 yards to a touchdown and, in a scene that is milked to the last tear, he dies with a grieving Pat O'Brien at his side. In 1941 he played Drake McHugh, an amiable bachelor whose legs are amputated by a sadistic doctor. In the film *King's Row*, Reagan awakens from the operation, discovers his legs are missing and cries out, "Where's the rest of me?" That scene established him as a star.

But the really big parts always eluded him. This haunted Reagan throughout his career. He had been exceedingly lucky to attain stardom while others with talents at least equal to his could not get in the front door, but although he extracted a lot of mileage from rather modest talents, Reagan always felt he had been unfairly disregarded. In his book he magnifies petty incidents into major causes, and the effect on his ego of the status-seeking games of Hollywood is nakedly apparent.

There was a special table at the M-G-M commissary where the reigning princes ate lunch: Cagney, Bogart, Dick Powell, Pat O'Brien and Frank McHugh. The established stars take the young man into their company and soon he is privileged to sit at the "in" table. But he pays a heavy price: as the small-town rube in Hollywood, Ronnie is the butt of merciless ribbing, a perfect target for the heavy-drinking, swaggering movie tough guys.

Every gene in him cries out that he is still Nelle Clyde's son and he is not cut out for the swinging, roistering Hollywood role. (At one point in his autobiography, Reagan says that he is an occasional light drinker, but basically he feels the world would be better off without liquor.) Nonetheless, he tries to run with the

movie crowd and they know how hard he is trying.
Actor Arthur Kennedy, who also served in the Army Air
Corps with Reagan, recalls that Reagan tried to throw
his drinks away when no one was looking, and director
Michael Curtiz remembers that in one Western movie
fellow actors, bemused by Reagan's obsession with
horses and cavalry, loosened the ties on his saddle and
Reagan landed in the dust when he tried to mount.

Except for two films, *King's Row* and *Knute Rockne,
All American,* artistic fulfillment eluded him. As Reagan
points out in his book, his other forty-eight films never
quite matched his impact in these two movies. In
Brother Rat, a 1938 comedy about military cadets,
Reagan felt that his part could have been a breakthrough for him but "Eddie Albert stole the honors—
and deservedly so." He appeared in a number of vehicles that launched lesser-known names—Eleanor
Parker in *Voice of the Turtle* and Richard Todd in *The
Hasty Heart.* Something or someone invariably popped
up to frustrate his career. He got a chance to make a
major movie, *Dark Victory,* with Bette Davis, George
Brent and Humphrey Bogart, but "It wasn't, however,
the rewarding experience it should have been." The
director interpreted his part as "the kind of fellow who
could sit in the girls' dressing room dishing the dirt
while they went on dressing in front of me. I had no
trouble seeing him in that role, but for myself I want to
think if I stroll through where the girls are short of
clothes, there will be a great scurrying about and taking
to cover."

When he appeared in a remake of *The Badman,*

Reagan was warned that he was playing with "an inveterate scene stealer," the late Wallace Beery. In one scene Reagan thought he had Beery, who was standing behind his horse while Reagan was free to maneuver at the horse's head. Reagan could not see how Beery could upstage him but "By the scene's end he was full face to the camera, which was virtually shooting over my shoulder. Like the old adage about forced romance: when it's inevitable, relax and enjoy it." Working in the same film with Lionel Barrymore, he recalls: "He was confined to his wheelchair at the time and he could whip that contrivance around on a dime. It's hard to smile in a scene when your foot has been run over and your shin is bleeding from a hubcap blow."

When Warner's asked Reagan to make *The Hasty Heart* in England, he refused at first. "I wanted to do an outdoor epic, and my complaint was that if I couldn't ride a horse on screen, I could ride my own off screen, but not if I went to England. Departure time was drawing near and I was sulking. The studio knew it couldn't shanghai me and drop me in England if my sulk persisted, so I was told in the friendliest way that the studio was looking for an outdoor property for me." Once in England, he spent his weekends touring the countryside in a chauffeur-driven Rolls-Royce. "As my homesickness grew," he recounts, "so did my resentment against the studio for cooking up the idea of an English picture. I hired the car and driver, putting the tab on the hotel bill, which I justified on the grounds that if I were home I'd have my own car to drive and besides, if Warner's wanted to unfreeze their refrigerated money, I'd help unfreeze a little extra. You are right; it was wrong and I'm ashamed of myself—but then, I'm not hungry and cold and 6,000 miles from home now."

Reagan's own account is of a man who relied on charm and a horse trader's sense to get his own way— and he generally succeeded by mixing ingenuousness and determination. But when others proved impervious to his charisma or exhibited the same competitiveness that infected Reagan, he was bewildered and hurt.

"He usually got aced out of the big roles," a Hollywood agent observed. "The studios couldn't sell him as a dynamic personality. He was nice enough but—maybe that was the trouble. To be a star of the first magnitude, you have to project a certain animal magnetism. Ronnie had good looks and a certain charm but he lacked that exciting quality. It's nothing to be ashamed of—very few actors have it. But Ronnie couldn't match the big guys like Bogart and Cagney. Now, William Holden, who is physically similar to Ronnie, got big parts year after year. Why not Ronnie? You tell me. Bill had that extra quirk that audiences wanted. Ronnie just couldn't sell that many tickets. You might say he had a low flame."

Ronnie may have been naïve but he was shrewd enough to sense the vibrations in Hollywood's paranoid atmosphere. He was edited out of scenes because the late Errol Flynn felt threatened by the young and handsome actor. Reagan noticed Flynn whispering to the director and, in the next scene, Reagan was stationed behind a row of taller actors and completely obscured. But Reagan, having quickly learned the rules of Hollywood's infighting, scuffed together a mound of dirt and climbed on it just as he gave his lines. Errol Flynn was a "beautiful piece of machinery," Reagan recalls, and he can't understand why Flynn felt insecure.

But the intense competition brought out an underlying anger in Reagan, anger that emerged when he felt frustrated and cramped by his eternal nice-guy role. In one film, it took three days to complete a fight sequence and Reagan was tired by the third day. His exasperation deepened each time the director told him to swing his fist a bit closer. Finally, he caught a stunt man flush on the jaw and knocked him down. "Naturally," Reagan recalls, "I felt terrible about the accident. At the same time, it was the first time I had ever knocked anyone out, and it was kind of nice knowing I could do it."

Reagan does not waste much sympathy and compassion on others, but nonetheless he remembers, nurses and treasures each snub and slight, fancied or real. He is unhappy because he has to take parts that lack style and he suffers exquisitely at the hands of incompetent directors, jealous actors and unappreciative producers. The bitchery in Hollywood is distastefully real, but in his autobiography Reagan seems to wallow in it as he tries to discover why the number one ranking always eluded him.

Perhaps the war had something to do with it, interrupting his career at its height. His autobiography goes to great lengths in justifying his role in the service as an officer who narrated training films at the old Hal Roach Studio in Culver City. As he explains that he was exempted from overseas duty because of poor eyesight,

Reagan adds, "Some people can't respect a uniform unless it's on a dead soldier." He was one of millions who
never got overseas but he feels compelled to observe
that he did vital service in the studio: "The military has
need of many things, in wartime especially, so there will
always be a need for specialized posts such as ours. None
has ever been more successful in fulfilling its mission
than was our wacky Hollywood stepchild. One of our
thirty-minute training films cut the training period for
aerial gunners by six weeks. Most of the millions of men
who never experienced combat had an almost reverent
feeling for the men who did face the enemy. Somehow
there was a feeling that you understood better than a
civilian what it was they were going through. In our
post this was heightened by the millions of feet of raw
film that came back to us from combat."

Reagan was discharged in August, 1945, and recalls:
"By the time I got out of the Army Air Corps, all I
wanted to do—in common with several million other
veterans—was to rest up awhile, make love to my wife,
and come up refreshed to a better job in an ideal world.
(As it came out, I was disappointed in all these postwar
ambitions . . .)" He had assumed that World War II was
"simply the immolation of the phoenix of human liber-
ties and that the bird of happiness would rise out of the
ashes and fly everywhere at once . . . I was wrong. I
learned that a thousand bucks under the table was the
formula for buying a new car. I learned that the real
estate squeeze was on for the serviceman. I discovered
that the rich had got just a little richer and a lot of the
poor had done a pretty good job of grabbing a quick

buck. I discovered that the world was almost the same and perhaps a little worse."

Having endured the war in a Culver City movie studio, a few miles from home, Reagan returned to civilian life and a $3,500-a-week job at Warner Brothers.

3

A Loss
of Innocence

After the war, life changed for Ronald Reagan, who
might be said to have suffered a loss of innocence. He
still had dreams and he still talked in an aw-shucks foot-
scuffing manner, but events in his personal and professional life shattered many of his illusions. When he entered the service in 1941 his time for stardom had come;
when he returned in 1945 it had passed—a new generation of moviegoers had come of age, although it took
years for reality to sink in. Meanwhile, another misfor-
tune befell him in the collapse of his marriage.

Ronald Reagan and Jane Wyman were married in 1940
after a romance that had the gossip columnists gushing:
both were stars, young, photogenic and apparently
eager to reap the publicity bonanza from what everyone
predicted would be an "ideal Hollywood marriage."
Every step of their romance, marriage and separation
was lovingly attended by the gossip mills, and the same
columnists clucked lugubriously when the marriage
ended in 1948. For eight years it was "Ronnie and Jane,"
toothy and smiling, who graced the fan magazine covers

as that loving Hollywood couple. They were introduced by columnist Louella Parsons, who invited them along on her *Hollywood Hotel* radio tour and who murmured approvingly when they started dating.

When he wed, Ronald Reagan was still the naïve, somewhat passive character he so often portrayed. His head was full of romantic Hollywood nonsense, and once he confessed in wide-eyed disappointment that kissing in front of cameras was something of a disappointment. In fact, he said, it was much more fun to kiss at a high-school picnic. On another occasion the studio arranged for him to escort the movies' "sweater girl," Lana Turner, to a premiere; Ronnie took her in a taxicab and was embarrassed to learn that everyone else traditionally arrived in a limousine to make the grand entrance complete.

Despite his native quickness, he was still a small-town boy in the big city, and it showed in many ways. When he and Jane Wyman wed, he was too thrilled by the attention from the press to understand that the exposure meant he had bartered away his privacy. Ronnie and Jane invited photographers to their home to record for posterity their newborn daughter and their moments of relaxation at poolside, Ronnie wearing an ascot (an affectation he quickly dropped) and Jane dressed in fetching white tennis shorts. When the fissures started to appear in the happy marital façade, it was not so easy to keep the press away after having allowed them to cover the happy events.

To this day Ronald Reagan refuses to discuss the breakup of his marriage, and he dismisses it with a few

lines in his autobiography. He was deeply wounded by
speculation in the columns that he was the injured party
and that Jane had walked out because he bored her. In
her divorce suit Miss Wyman gave the usual perfunctory reasons: Ronnie was too involved in the Guild and
in politics, and she could not share his interest. There
were suggestions that Jane Wyman, a gregarious and
talented actress with a lusty vocabulary, wanted her
freedom after eight years of marriage to a man who remained an ingenue in his thirties. The Reagans had two
children: Maureen, who was born in 1941, and an
adopted son, Michael, who was born in 1945.

Years later, at a *Photoplay* magazine awards dinner,
he revealed his resentment of the press for intruding on
his privacy. "The movie industry has suffered from irresponsible journalism," he told a banquet hall full of
movie stars and journalists, "and the irresponsible press
has given the world the idea that everybody in Hollywood is immoral or crazy . . .

"The real Hollywood isn't the conception of Hollywood that is being given the world . . . by gossip columnists whose only stock in trade is, literally, back-fence
gossip. It is shameful."

Perhaps new performers need personal attention from
the press, he suggested, but established stars who don't
need publicity should be considered off-limits.

"I have always felt actors should answer questions
and have publicity only about actual movie trade news,
not on their private lives. They don't sell Ford cars by
telling what Henry Ford eats for breakfast, do they?
What I do or don't do is of no concern to the reader. I

don't think it is news as to whom I had out to dinner last night."

Most performers with any degree of sophistication don't bother to dignify Hollywood journalism with a rebuttal. When he was going up, Reagan enjoyed the press's uncritical acceptance of him as a totally admirable celebrity. When the first crack had appeared in the image, and the columnists had printed their meager speculation about his divorce, he blamed the press for violating the privacy that he had given up years ago. He knew the rules in Hollywood and, having traded away his privacy for professional gain, he sounded like a crybaby when he lamented the injustice of it.

Reagan attacked the press at a time when the prewar generation of stars—Robert Taylor, Errol Flynn, Tyrone Power and Jimmy Stewart—were going out of fashion. Young moviegoers were not buying tickets to see Ronnie Reagan either; they wanted a change in direction, and Reagan, although still young, was caught in a generation gap. He had come of age, professionally, while Hollywood was making two kinds of films: the social message picture in which John Garfield or Jimmy Stewart speculated on how wonderful America would be if we could get rid of Edward Arnold and his reactionary newspapers, and the purely escapist fare of white telephones, ornately dressed chorines and Betty Grable dancing with John Payne. After the war the days of uncritical acceptance had ended, along with the public's interest in the shining-eyed, virginal heroes portrayed by Reagan.

If Americans craved escapism, there was the lure of a

new medium, television; for sophisticated entertainment, they could see foreign films. The prewar style of film-making faded as audiences became obsessed with a new realism, symbolized by the ashcan and the grimy undershirt. The new stars of the Fifties were shaggy and inarticulate heroes like Marlon Brando and James Dean, while Ronnie Reagan was still rooted in the era when nobody in the movies sweated or scratched.

Reagan refused to confront reality and, like many other stars who defied the inevitable decline, he kept waiting for that one important movie role that would reestablish his importance. He kept up the self-delusion; he was not out of work, simply "between pictures." While waiting for a comeback he declined offers to work in television, and he also turned down a number of Broadway offers. He was determined to make it big in Hollywood.

With time on his hands "between pictures," Reagan became increasingly involved in the tight little world that comprises Hollywood's community life. He was still an incessant joiner and meeting-goer. He attended meetings of the Screen Actors Guild and soon he was taking an active part. He loved the speechmaking and the parliamentary maneuvering, and he could devote considerable time to the SAG. He started rising in the Guild's hierarchy and eventually he was elected president of the 15,000-member union, a position he held for six terms. As president he performed essentially as a public relations representative of the actors while a permanent Guild staff handled the union's administrative affairs.

After his discharge in 1945 Reagan became active in politics, an interest he inherited from his father. As a child of the Depression, having left Eureka in 1932, he had voted enthusiastically for Franklin D. Roosevelt and the New Deal. "I was a near-hopeless, hemophilic liberal," Reagan says of the period between his discharge and the 1947 Hollywood investigation by the House Committee on Un-American Activities. He scoffed at those who worried about Communist penetration in the movies and considered them reactionary alarmists.

"About this time," he declared, "I had the uncomfortable consciousness of being unusually naïve. Something seemed wrong—and I wasn't exactly sure what it was. But one of the few advantages of naïveté lies in the fact that you don't have too much mental rubbish. You can approach a fresh notion with the delight of a child snatching up a bright new dime. Preconceived ideas and pear-shaped prejudices appear crystal clear to the ingenuous."

The political education of Ronald Reagan was painful and slow. By his own recollection, his doctrinaire liberal assumptions first were shaken during his wartime service when he saw a self-serving bureaucracy at work. He observed that one incompetent secretary was promoted, and thus removed from her assignment, because it would have required too much red tape to fire her outright. After his discharge Reagan started making patriotic speeches, and one evening in the spring of 1946 he got heavy applause when he condemned fascism, but the audience sat in stony silence when he criticized communism.

From 1945 to 1947 he joined a number of liberal organizations, like the United World Federalists and Americans for Democratic Action, and also two groups on the Far Left, the Hollywood Independent Citizens Committee for the Arts, Sciences and Professions and the Hollywood chapter of the American Veterans Committee. He resigned from HICCASP in 1946 after a stormy meeting in which he was attacked as a "Fascist" because he endorsed an anti-Communist resolution. He left the veterans' group in 1947 after discovering that a decision to picket a studio had been made by only 73 members out of a total of 1,300. "Light was dawning in some obscure region in my head," Reagan explained. "I was beginning to see the seamy side of liberalism. . . . Something the liberal will have to explain and stand trial for is his inability to see the Communist as he truly is and not as some kind of Peck's Bad Boy of liberalism who is basically all right but just a bit overboard and rough-edged."

In his ultraliberal period, Reagan saw Communists and fellow travelers take over meetings when the general membership failed to attend, pass resolutions without debate and call strikes in the name of the entire membership. When Reagan and others protested these tactics (copied so faithfully years later by the Birch Society), they were called "Fascist scum" and "lackeys." He quickly resigned from Communist-front organizations when it dawned on him that communism was more than a political movement. Reagan had always uttered the conventional liberal rhetoric and Hollywood's acceptable shorthand phrases. Like much of the movie colony, Ronald Reagan had not arrived at liberalism by working out his own position; he simply struck a pose. But even in his most "hemophilic" period, his instinctive conservatism emerged whenever anyone mentioned the income tax, which he considered discriminatory.

The more he learned about the Far Left, the more embattled he became. The fellow travelers knew they could usually neutralize Reagan by goading him into a temper tantrum. They saw Reagan as vulnerable in that he was self-righteous and rigid; and he was ridiculed mercilessly. But one day he got an anonymous telephone threat and the ribbing no longer seemed funny. Reagan got a police permit to carry a pistol, and grimly shook off any suggestion that someone might have played a practical joke on him. By that time Hollywood had been staggering under a succession of bloody jurisdictional strikes, and the studios were contending with labor racketeers as well as Communists. When the House Committee on Un-American Activities investigated the movies, no one was surprised that Reagan appeared as a friendly witness.

While Hollywood was recovering from its Red scare, Reagan got an unusual request in 1951 from Director Mervyn LeRoy. A young M-G-M actress, Nancy Davis, was concerned that leftist literature mailed unsolicited to her apartment might jeopardize her career. Reagan asked the guild's investigator to check. Apparently there was a mix-up in names, but Miss Davis was not being blacklisted as a result of the mistake. Reagan offered to telephone the actress with the news, but·LeRoy said the lady really needed reassurance, and suggested dinner. Reagan knew the old Hollywood game: it isn't unusual for ambitious actresses to seek out stars on a variety of pretexts. But LeRoy insisted. "I figured she was a little starlet from the studio," Reagan recalled. "When I telephoned her, I made it clear that I had an early studio call the next day so we had to make it an early dinner."

Miss Davis realized that Reagan was fortifying himself against the possibility of a tedious evening, and she told him that an early dinner was fine with her because she had an early call too. Apparently, it took heavy persuading by Reagan to convince Miss Davis that her career was safe; after dinner on the Sunset Strip, they went to a nightclub and sat through two Sophie Tucker performances. Miss Davis had scored a social coup: she had been out with the president of the Screen Actors Guild and they had made plans to meet again. Thus began a friendship that culminated in marriage March 4, 1952.

Nancy Davis is a tiny brunette with wide-set brown eyes and a determined smile, who made it clear from the start that she was not another "little starlet." Doors opened magically for her in Hollywood, which is usually awed by anyone with a correct social background. Her father is Dr. Loyal Davis, a wealthy Chicago surgeon with emphatically conservative views, and her mother a former Broadway actress, Edith Luckett. The actress Nazimova was her godmother, and Nancy Davis was interested in theater as a child. After graduating from Girls Latin School in Chicago and Smith College in

Northampton, Massachusetts, she appeared in summer stock with ZaSu Pitts and later in a Broadway play, *The Lute Song*, with Mary Martin and Yul Brynner.

"I was never obsessed with becoming a movie actress," Miss Davis recalls, "and I was too used to the theater to be stage-struck. I came to Hollywood because I didn't want to return to Chicago and lead the life of a post-deb." At M-G-M she usually was cast as the expectant mother in family-type melodramas, and today she insists that she cannot even recall the titles of her film credits. One of her last films was *Hell Cats of the Navy*, in which Ronald Reagan starred.

Since her husband's rise in politics Nancy Reagan has emerged in the California press as an adoring and dutiful Super-Wife. When she accompanied her husband in 1966, Nancy Reagan stood at his side, tilted her head upward and gazed worshipfully at Ronnie throughout his speeches. Greeting each other before television cameras, the Reagans embraced rapturously, as if they had not seen each other a few hours before at breakfast. In public they acted as if they were honeymooning, not campaigning. "Ronnie is my hero," Nancy told interviewers unblushingly, "and it may sound corny, but I would be happy to live anywhere as long as I was with Ronnie and the children."

In newspaper and television interviews it became clear that Nancy had a script as carefully crafted as Reagan's basic speech. Invariably she repeated the same set pieces, word for word: she and Ronnie never dreamed about a political career; she never considered the governor's mansion let alone the White House; she and Ronnie are just folks who prefer the quiet life to the Hollywood rounds.

Despite their passion for privacy, they have permitted reporters and cameramen to record their family activities for TV documentaries and Sunday sections. One documentary, simply entitled *Nancy*, devoted most of an hour to showing Mrs. Reagan shopping at a supermarket, selecting a gown, walking around their ranch and giving a pool party for her son's friends. The Reagans have not hesitated to display their two photogenic children, Patricia Ann, fourteen, and Ronald Prescott Reagan, nine. The family photographs beautifully: outdoorsy, clean-limbed and casual. In 1966, campaign advertisements subtly reinforced the idea that the Reagans were Young Marrieds. The official family photograph, used in his campaign literature, showed Reagan with his present family. The children of his marriage to Jane Wyman, Mrs. Maureen (Reagan) Sills, twenty-seven, and Michael Reagan, twenty-four, were excluded; in fact, they were kept away from the press during the campaign. The older children's exclusion from the campaign photo bothered Reagan's advisers, who feared the omission might bring up questions about Reagan's earlier marriage. So Michael and Maureen were inserted in the background of the original photograph but, despite the photo editor's artifice, it is obviously a retouched picture.

The Reagans' permanent home is in Pacific Palisades, a suburb in West Los Angeles, where they have a modern hilltop home atop winding San Onofre Drive. From their front window they have a broad view of the Los

Angeles Basin, which seems to rise just beyond the rim of their swimming pool. The house is pleasantly and tastefully furnished with indoor plants, an all-electric kitchen and a modest library. There is one homy, Midwestern touch in the living room: the piano near the window is covered with photographs of celebrities and politicians, including Dwight Eisenhower, Richard Nixon, Barry Goldwater and Nazimova. Most of the house has the ordered look of a museum and the visitor senses an air of impersonality and blandness as though it were a television set where a company was filming a series about a suburban family.

The all-electric kitchen came from General Electric, the corporation that resurrected Reagan's career. In 1954 GE was looking for a television master of ceremonies for its new anthology series. It also wanted a celebrity to act as GE's representative, tour its plants and meet its employees. Someone like Ed Sullivan would have been ideal: an unobtrusive yet prestigious "name" rather than a "talent," who would be welcome week after week in millions of homes. What GE wanted is not easy to find: a personality who could act as host, visit company employees and introduce products without descending to obvious hucksterism.

By that time Reagan was living from guest spot to guest spot on television, and he was nearly $18,000 in debt. He was so hard-pressed that he took a two-week job as an M.C. at the Last Frontier Hotel in Las Vegas, where he performed a routine kidding himself for not being able to sing, dance or tell jokes.

In Reagan, General Electric found a perfect host. The

GE show gave Reagan an eight-year course in the art of public relations, and he excelled at it. He toured all of GE's 135 plants and met most of the 250,000 employees. Sometimes he walked miles along assembly lines to shake hands with workers on the night shift, and he estimates that he spent nearly two years just in touring plants. Much of the traveling time was made necessary by Reagan's aversion to flying; he insisted on touring by train or car. When he walked through the dining car everyone noticed the handsome celebrity. He usually ate alone at his table and, when his meal was over, quickly returned to his private compartment. After years of public exposure, he did not want to meet strangers in his off hours too.

At first his public relations work consisted of hand-shaking tours and a perfunctory pitch for free enterprise. Gradually, the speech shifted emphasis as he came into contact with top-level corporation executives. He was impressed by the no-nonsense achievers in the business world and their business viewpoint meshed with his budding conservatism. Now he responded to his new environment, looking at national problems from the perspective of the beleaguered businessmen, and an anti-government theme ran through his speeches: unresponsive federal bureaucrats were stifling free enterprise, and only an aroused citizenry could roll back the tide of "creeping socialism." Perhaps determined to atone for his past errors, Reagan became a full-time apostle for the conservative business viewpoint. GE rewarded him with an annual salary of $125,000, later raising it to $165,000 as Reagan acquired a part ownership in GE

Theater. Unblushingly, he described his sponsor as "a vast corporation but as human as the corner grocer."

His speech was going over so well at club luncheons and employee meetings that he decided to build it up. His bitter indictment of government got dangerously specific, however, when he criticized the Tennessee Valley Authority as an example of government mismanagement. Angry letters flowed into General Electric. Eventually, Reagan got a roundabout message: GE was doing $50 million worth of business with TVA, and his attacks were jeopardizing the company's relations with the federal agency. But there was no direct word from the top. Ralph Cordiner, president of GE, who had approved the hiring of Reagan and advised him to "work out a philosophy for yourself" as a GE speechmaker, insisted, when Reagan telephoned, that it was his responsibility to handle complaints about Reagan's speeches. But the actor, sensing discomfiture in Cordiner's voice, asked if he could make his speech just as effectively without mentioning TVA. "It would make my job easier," Cordiner conceded. Reagan deleted the reference and squared it with his conscience by noting that he was acting in the interest of a thousand employees whose jobs were threatened by his criticism of TVA. In 1962 General Electric asked Reagan to limit his speeches to conventional huckstering of its products, but Reagan liked the idea of speaking out on profound issues. He refused and, twenty-four hours later, the company canceled the *GE Theater*, contending that the show was declining in the ratings because of stiff competition from the TV Western, *Bonanza*. After ending his relationship with GE, Reagan signed on with the U. S. Borax Corporation as the host for a Western series, *Death Valley Days*.

His eight years with GE had given him experience in public relations that would have been the envy of any politician. On tour, with his trained ear for audiences, he became aware of a great unease at the grass roots. Americans in every region felt powerless and frustrated; they sensed that something was wrong with the American reality, that government had become so intricately webbed with special interests and cross-purposes that perhaps no one could control it or even comprehend its complexity. Reagan could identify with this unease and, more important, he could articulate it. He and Nancy, who helped him with research, read newspapers, magazines and the *Congressional Record* and fitted appropriate pieces into his speech. Gradually, "The Speech" took shape as Reagan honed and polished it for eight years. When he delivered it on national television October 27, 1964, it stood as the culmination of all the forces that had shaped Ronald Reagan's life and attitudes.

4

The "Againster" Tradition

The Californian is a notorious "againster" who votes against rather than for candidates—and the state's political history encourages this negative tradition. In the absence of overriding and clear-cut issues (and most California campaigns are too homogenized and obscured with platitudes to present definitive alternatives), the voter makes his choice for personal and subjective reasons. A candidate's appearance, stage presence and personal style are occasionally the difference between victory and defeat.

A postcard-sized photo of Richard Milhous Nixon contributed to his humiliating loss in 1962; and he left the state after chastising the press and characterizing California politics as "a can of worms." The photo showed Nixon, shadow-jowled, muffin-faced and narrow-eyed, and asked: "Would you buy a used car from this man?" Two years later Pierre Salinger, swarthy, stubby and a perpetual gnawer of cigars, lost an election he was expected to win handily. The voters, many of them from other states, considered Salinger, who is a native Cali-

fornian, a "carpetbagger." Now it is obvious that Nixon
and Salinger were not defeated *solely* because of a post-
card and a meaningless phrase. But somehow these inci-
dental touches summed up a general feeling against
both men: the voter knew, or rather felt, that something
was wrong, something he couldn't define but nevertheless sensed. And the California voter is often right—for
the wrong reasons.

Everything militates against his getting the information he needs in order to make a rational choice; so he
decides on the basis of irrational feelings. Nevertheless
he has shown over the years an intuitive grasp of political reality. First he votes out one party, then the other,
thus keeping the politicians in a constant state of
anxiety—and, given the voter's frustrations and the system's inhibitions, this is perhaps the best of all possible
situations.

California politics traditionally are individualistic;
the man, not the party, is the issue. Through the years
this custom has evolved into "the star system," a non-
system which has an illogic of its own. Under the star
system, alliances and loyalties are formed around personalities with little or no regard for party or ideology.
Although the professionals have tried to dismiss the system as an unfortunate consequence of the Hollywood
influence, there are signs that it is spreading across the
United States. The men on the ascendancy in politics—
John Lindsay, Charles Percy, the Kennedy brothers—
capitalize on an appeal that transcends identifying
labels.

California's personalized style of politics is breaking

down the old loyalties of party, precinct and ward as
voters become more sophisticated, more mobile, more
"politicalized." The old ties of labor union, ethnic bloc
and geography are dissolving. The change reflects, in
part, the voter's (correct) suspicion that most of the
dogma and doctrine of conventional American politics
is so much rhetoric; that the labels "liberal" and "conservative" are obscured by the momentous and unantic-
ipated problems of the Sixties; that doctrinaire assumptions stultify the public servant's attempt to confront
and solve problems.

Then there is television. It has banished forever the
candidate as a remote and oracular figure, who appears
at July Fourth barbecues and is seen from a dis-
tance in the shadows of a torch-lit rally. Everything pre-
ceding television is as dated as the tedious and costly
whistle-stop campaign. The tube makes or breaks the
candidate. It makes ideology and party label seem even
more like excess baggage as it brings the campaigner
into the home and gives the voter a chance to study his
personality and appearance. If a candidate can sway
millions on television he doesn't need the party; it needs
him. Thus a young senator with an ambiguous record,
John Fitzgerald Kennedy, became President; the voter
sensed an activist blessed not only with youthful vigor
but a sense of history.

In California, where everything seems new and
strange, where new communities spring up overnight,
where few know their neighbors, television provides
that sense of community that the newcomer never
missed until he left home. It has reinforced the star sys-

tem by obliterating everything but the individual. When the average Californian gets home after the daily grind, television reaches out to him and softens that sense of social isolation that afflicts so many in the Golden State. In his home he exercises a Godlike control of his environment: a flick of the wrist and the world's troubles, riots, war and crime, parade before his eyes; another flick—situation comedy. After he becomes addicted to it he neither realizes nor cares that the medium can manipulate him too.

Because of television, politics in California are more individualistic than ever. "There is no political machine here," goes the old saying, "just a lot of moving parts." As a result of the personality cult, California elections are manic-depressive, given to wide swings that are fascinating but unpredictable. In one year, a school bond issue fails by 1,000,000 votes; in the next, it passes by 1,300,000. The political mortality rate is frighteningly high (perhaps that is the Californian's way of keeping the professionals honest), and the new face often feels like a minnow dropped into a pool of sharks. The legion of the fallen in California is a list of once-potent names: Richard Nixon, William F. Knowland, Murray Chotiner, Paul Ziffren, George Christopher, Goodwin J. Knight, Pierre Salinger and Pat Brown. California likes big winners, and a defeat is a mark of Cain; consequently, the worst epithet in California politics is "loser." A political defeat consigns the victim to an outer darkness as total as if he had stopped paying his light and telephone bills.

The political parties reflect the anxious and volatile

atmosphere. Republican Earl Warren is the only man to win the governorship of California three times in this century. He is revered by thousands of Democrats as a progressive and humanitarian leader, but the conservative wing of the California GOP considers him a renegade. Mayor Sam Yorty of Los Angeles, a conservative Democrat who supported Nixon against Kennedy in 1960, is popular with Republicans and hated by regular Democrats. U. S. Senator Thomas Kuchel, a conservative turned moderate-liberal, is branded a Judas by some of his fellow Republicans, but he has won reelection with considerable help from Democrats.

The Democrats of California are a classic example of confused identity-seeking. The party has elected only two governors in this century, although it has held a registration edge since the Thirties. Registered Democrats currently outnumber the opposition by 1 million, a margin that has held steady since the Forties, but there is only one Democrat (Attorney General Thomas Lynch) who holds statewide office in 1968. Many Californians like to register Democratic and vote Republican—or at least it seems that way, because approximately one out of every five Democrats is really a conservative, a Dixiecrat or a descendant of "Okies" and "Arkies." Ideologically, they would feel more comfortable in the conservative wing of the Republican party, but they cling to the Democratic label, and so the majority party's edge is more illusion than reality.

Why do they remain? Traditional ties? The New Deal? Probably, because the Democratic party is more like an ill-assorted, wrangling family than a tight political organization. The Republicans in California exude social prestige; they are bright and buttoned-down; but despite window-dressing they project a restrictive country club atmosphere: overwhelmingly white, Anglo-Saxon Protestant, suburban, professional, peanut-butter-and-jelly, blue-haired ladies munching finger sandwiches. The Democrats are more like the United Nations, taking in everybody under their patchwork tent: Negroes from the ghettos, Mexican-Americans in the barrios of East Los Angeles, shaggy intellectuals off the campus, wealthy liberal Jews, low-income whites and gray-haired pensioners.

In this century the Republicans have overcome a registration handicap by matching the Democrats in promises and surpassing them in efficiency and organization. To win statewide, the Republicans must hold 90 per cent of the GOP vote and peel off approximately 25 per cent of the opposition's. It is not an impossible task because of the pivotal conservative bloc in the Democratic party. Until 1966 the Republicans won by offering progressive and activist government under chief executives like Warren and Goodwin J. Knight, who appealed to Democrats because they built schools, roads and hospitals, pioneered unemployment insurance, old age pensions and workmen's compensation. By accomplishing what the Democrats promised, they earned the undying enmity of conservatives in their own party. In modern times the moderate-liberal wing of the Republican party had submerged the conservatives, but a series of feuds weakened the moderate majority and the conservatives moved into the leadership vacuum created by Nixon's departure in 1962.

The Democrats' heterogeneity is a weakness as well as a strength. They cannot rally their blocs with a single unifying program or slogan. California Republicans have a better record for turning out on Election Day; they are better educated, better motivated, more community-minded and more likely to volunteer for political chores. The volunteer effort by Republicans in the comfortable suburbs ringing Los Angeles is a marvel of effectiveness, and the tightly knit, well-organized county headquarters can mobilize battalions of elderly and indefatigable ladies to carry petitions and ring doorbells. "Never knock the ladies," says U. S. Senator George Murphy, who benefited from their help; "they can cover a block like a pack of beavers." The Republican party can further dilute the opposition's edge with help from the press. Nearly 90 per cent of California's newspapers are Republican-oriented. Although newspaper endorsements are no longer crucial in the television era, a sympathetic press helps immeasurably in a limited area, like a legislative or congressional district, where a newspaper is the chief opinion-maker.

While the Republicans easily turn out their faithful in the suburbs (especially in Southern California, where more than two-thirds of the population resides), the Democrats cannot mobilize ethnic groups on a precinct basis as in the East and Midwest, chiefly because they have no year around structure for nurturing the grass roots. To the party's natural allies, the poor, foreign-born, uneducated Mexican-Americans and Negroes, the election sometimes becomes meaningless competition between two propertied white men ("Anglos" to Mexican-Americans), and the issues are cloudy. To roll up a vote in the ghettos and barrios, the party relies on labor unions. But in the Sixties the unions have been afflicted with affluence, and the rank-and-file, enjoying overtime and fringe benefits, are more interested in enjoying the status quo than in registering foreigners and Negroes. It took a monumental defeat in 1966 to make a painfully obvious fact clear to California Democrats: the labor unions no longer can "deliver" the vote.

Before 1966 the Democrats relied heavily on the California Democratic Council, the largest volunteer organization in the nation. The Council's club movement, inspired by Adlai Stevenson, resurrected the Democratic party in the Fifties and helped take the edge off the GOP's advantage in organization, money and expertise. But the club movement has fallen into disarray because of the war in Vietnam, and pressures from professionals who were embarrassed by the Council's ultra-liberal resolutions. The Republicans have their volunteer groups, too: the Young Republicans, California Republican Assembly, United Republicans of California and Federated Women's Clubs. And occasionally their party hierarchy is also embarrassed by volunteers, who get hung up on income tax and fluoridated water. But it is the volunteer in both parties who gives politics in California a social conscience as well as a special flavor of lively idealism. The volunteer spirit often comes to fullest flower, ironically, in the cause of a doomed candidate: the liberals for the star-crossed Stevenson of the Fifties, the conservatives for Goldwater in the Sixties. Again it was the star system at work; others have proclaimed Stevensonian and Goldwaterite principles, but something in the chemistry of these two men captured the imagination of the grass roots.

The star system began in 1911, when a towering progressive, Republican Hiram Johnson, set out to break the political domination of the railroads. Johnson rooted out every vestige of the old spoils system, and California, which had been shocked by political scandals and murders, elected Johnson governor and later U. S. Senator. California adopted "direct democracy": the "people" acquired broad legislative powers of initiative, referendum and recall; the official parties were consigned housekeeping roles, limited to a biennial meeting, passage of a forgettable platform and adjournment; the practice of holding party conventions to pick candidates was abolished and California has held direct primaries ever since. In keeping with Johnson's reforms, California adopted cross-filing, which permitted candidates to seek nomination in both parties. Until 1959 the California ballot did not include party designation, so determined were Californians to eliminate bosses and machines. The Democrats, who won the state in 1958, abolished cross-filing but the suspicion of parties and politicians remains strong.

California has no bosses, no Tammany Halls, very few spoils. But somehow the antiseptically clean system has not worked quite to perfection. An army of image makers and analysts, public-relations experts, computer technicians, pollsters and campaign managers has supplanted the old boss. It is doubtful whether the voice of "the people" can filter through this professional screen any more effectively than it did in the bad old days. In

the new non-system, the professional has taken over the
business of politics. It costs big money, and it gets more
expensive each year, to run for office in California. A
respectable statewide campaign costs at least $1 million
for television and radio, newspaper advertisements, direct mail, telephone solicitation, billboards, pamphlets
and bumper stickers. You can hire a campaign manager,
who will handle everything from money-raising to
doorbell-ringing, for $50,000. A professional firm in San
Francisco will circulate your initiative petitions for fifty
cents a signature. The technicians prosper in California
because there are no viable party organizations to
handle campaign chores. A Californian who has decided to run solicits funds, hires a manager, patches together a staff and campaigns—all independent of the
party structure. By the next election his staff is scattered
among several campaigns. And the voters are equally
elusive; Californians change homes as frequently as
they do cars. In 1964 there were precincts in Southern
California where more than half of the residents had
moved since the last election. Californians, in their rush
up the status ladder, seem to move into new communities almost before the concrete is dry on the latest
freeway.

Because of the electorate's size and mobility, and the
costs involved in reaching it, a serious candidate (unless
he is exceedingly wealthy) cannot afford to run independently of big contributors, who represent essentially
the same interests that Hiram Johnson tried to eliminate. (When Goodwin Knight was challenged for the
governorship by Senator William F. Knowland, the

governor found his campaign sources had mysteriously dried up; so he ran for the U. S. Senate instead, and the California voters got so fed up with the Republicans' musical chairs that they kicked them all out of office.)

California's tradition of "direct democracy" is something less than that because special interests, rather than the people, have learned how to exploit it. Anyone who can raise $2 million can propose a constitutional amendment, hire a staff of experts and put on a successful initiative campaign. Thus the State Constitution has become the target of special interests who feel no qualms about subjecting complicated legislative matters to the passions of an electorate that is often misled by billboards and radio jingles.

As a result, a half-century of reform politics has not made a significant change in the essential power relationships that Hiram Johnson confronted in 1911. California simply altered the rules of the game for railroads, utilities, oil companies, landholders, liquor interests and racetrack owners. They hire experts who use the shrewd sell to win elections in California. The only hedge against the manipulators is the intuitive skepticism of the California voter, who remains, for good reason, an "againster." Although he can be seduced by personalities and slogans, the turnover is rapid because of the welter of competing interests; each exotic promoter who springs out of the woodwork has a short hour in the California sun and then returns to obscurity.

The Californian usually votes for the candidate who is least threatening to him, a decision based on what he considers his pocketbook interests. When government acts in his economic interest—guaranteeing security as well as opportunity with pensions, disability pay and free higher education—the voter sees it as progress. But in the affluent Sixties the wage earner no longer identifies with the poor, and efforts to relieve their hardships are interpreted as pandering to "special interests." He is righteously indignant about squandering his tax dollars for people he considers unable to rise by their own bootstraps. On the other hand, he equates *his* interest with good government and "the people."

Whoever can make this subtle pitch most successfully, appealing to class interests but masking that appeal in vague moralization, preempts the Good Guy role. Confronted with the mind-boggling length of the ballot, obscure names, initiatives, bond issues and all the complications of "direct democracy," the voter retains only his instinctive distrust and a fleeting sense of what makes up the Good Guy.

Thus California politics abound with opportunities and temptations for self-dramatizers and oversimplifiers, who rely on charisma instead of character. The intricate questions are reduced to black-and-white slogans and personalities, and everything else is remote and ill-defined. The successful politician knows that the voter does not have time to reflect on the multitude of state problems, that the real division between Democrats and Republicans is about even, and therefore he angles his appeal toward the crucial 5 per cent who are uncommitted. He must read the anxieties and aspirations of that 5 per cent, who switch sides not only in each election but in each contest on the ballot. He can appeal to their instinctive mistrust by making the opposition the issue—i.e., the Bad Guy.

Armed with polls, socioeconomic profiles and computer data, he senses California's mood—liberal in economic terms, conservative in social issues—and tailors his message accordingly. He projects a vision of the future that can be evoked with a slogan, but he is leery of spelling it out to voters who are skeptical of neatly labeled answers. To win, he avoids doctrinaire blueprints that box him into an ideological corner; instead, he projects an image of a pragmatic and tough-minded problem solver.

As in Presidential campaigning, he must position himself in the middle and demonstrate the opposition to be "outside of the mainstream." The mainstream is becoming harder to define in California, which reflects the national anxiety over Vietnam and riots at home. Because of pressures from left and right, the old two-party system is breaking up, and the change is more evident in California than any other state. The change began in 1964 when Barry Goldwater shook loose the traditional political moorings, and it was accelerated by a fair-housing battle, riots in the cities, protests on campuses and fragmentation of the Democratic party.

The polarization that began in 1964 continues four years later and, in the turbulence, political scientists detect a massive sea change in American politics: a new, post-Goldwater conservative movement. As the liberal dreams fade under the impact of Vietnam, black power and an unpopular Democratic President, the Right has capitalized on the disillusionment that followed the assassination of John F. Kennedy on November 22, 1963. The liberals and moderates remain disenchanted and leaderless. As a result of the change in America's direction, Ronald Reagan has emerged as a serious candidate for the Presidency because he offers answers and, equally important, because he is able to articulate them. Unlike President Johnson, who cannot communicate effectively, Reagan can inspire as well as convince, and he excels on television. Because his eloquence washes out doubts about his program and his commitment, Ronald Reagan has become the Right's answer to the despair that settled on America after November 22, 1963. Within a year of the President's death, Ronald Reagan began his undeclared campaign for the White House. The first step was the governorship of California.

5

A Swing
to the Right

In order to fully understand Reagan's success in 1966, however, it is necessary to further examine the political events of 1964. Both Barry Goldwater's primary victory that year and George Murphy's successful race for the Senate seat in the general election were essential elements in the rise of Ronald Reagan.

The primary began in a mood of despair; few Californians had much zest for campaigning so soon after the assassination of John F. Kennedy. With the national mood tending to rally around the man who succeeded the President, Barry Goldwater knew that a Republican defeat in 1964 was virtually a foregone conclusion. But other conservatives, sensing subterranean political shifts, believed that a reaction was forming in response to the civil rights turmoil. For years the question of race had divided conservatives North and South but, Goldwater's advisers reasoned, white resistance to Negro militance could wipe out the regional differences that divided conservatives. If not in 1964, then later. Meanwhile, Goldwater's nomination would give conservatives control of the GOP machinery for the first time in years—and permit them to exercise a veto power over the 1968 Presidential nominee. The Goldwater candidacy was far more than an exercise in futility; it was a concerted and well-calculated move by a minority sect in the minority party to move the entire spectrum of American politics several degrees to the Right. And it worked.

But for Goldwater to get the nomination, he had to win California's primary. If he could carry a large industrial state like California, it would demonstrate to skeptical party leaders the extent of his strength at the grass roots. Goldwater's opposition, with a few exceptions, was halfhearted and fragmented—the liberals and moderates could not work up enthusiasm to fight for the GOP nomination in "a Democratic year."

Governor Nelson Aldrich Rockefeller of New York sensed that the Goldwaterites really wanted a lien on the GOP's future, and he amassed a multimillion-dollar war chest to stop them. He knew that California would be the chief 1964 primary battleground but Rockefeller, despite ability and wealth, was handicapped in California, where Goldwater was considered a neighbor and Rockefeller a Republican heretic.

Since 1962, when Nixon left California, a quiet despair had settled on the state's GOP. The moderates were too stunned by the Nixon fiasco to check the conservative onslaught, and Goldwater's campaign began the day Nixon left. While moderates brooded, the conservatives took over the volunteer organizations: the California Republican Assembly, the Young Republicans, United

Republicans of California and the grass-roots women's clubs. These plums fell like ripe fruit into their laps and, with tenacity, skill and guile, the Right started putting together a Goldwater Presidential boom. They also moved in on the state and county Central Committees. Constantly, they exploited the old Populist fears: Rockefeller was a hated symbol of Eastern wealth, international finance and the Establishment. Moreover, there were whispers about his divorce and remarriage to a woman who had yielded custody of her four children to marry the governor.

Throughout the primary, this subliminal campaign haunted Rockefeller. Most Republicans in California preferred someone else as the liberal-moderate alternative to Goldwater. But the others—Nixon, Henry Cabot Lodge and William Scranton—were not listed on the ballot. It had to be Rockefeller or Goldwater, and the very mention of their names stirred fratricidal impulses among California Republicans.

Rockefeller was so unpopular in California that he had to be propped up with prestigious names. Most of the state's illustrious Establishment figures backed the New York governor—the Chandlers, Sutros, Darts, Firestones, Rowans and Fleischhackers. To bolster his credentials as a "real Republican," Rockefeller enlisted the top GOP votegetter in California, U.S. Senator Tom Kuchel, as his campaign chairman. And his supporters assembled a Rockefeller convention slate that was a masterpiece of geographical, ethnic and professional balance to demonstrate that the governor had appeal for all groups.

The public-relations firm of Spencer-Roberts, active since 1960, attracted Rockefeller's attention after engineering a number of upsets in heavily Democratic districts. In 1963 New York National Committeeman George Hinman asked them to analyze the governor's chances in California. "We reported back," said Stu Spencer, "that the Nixon people had done a job on the governor since 1960. He was strictly bad news in California. Not even the Dark Ages, the *Ice Ages*. The Rockefeller people paid us and said nothing."

A few weeks later, Spencer-Roberts was asked to handle the California primary for Rockefeller. They accepted after a month of reflection, having turned down an offer from the Goldwater organization. "We figured," said Spencer, "that with Rockefeller we had no place to go but up. We realized we couldn't capture the party machinery for Rockefeller—worse yet, we couldn't even rely on the party to remain neutral—so we built our own organization from the ground up. For weeks we had trouble trying to get a volunteer thing going. How do you jazz people about the cause of moderation? Goldwater had a corner on the volunteer talent. You have to hand it to the Birchers: they are great little workers. Our volunteers just couldn't match their energy."

Spencer and Roberts deployed 600 professional telephone solicitors to make certain the Governor and Mrs. Rockefeller got a warm reception at Disneyland. More than 5,000 Californians fidgeted in line at the Disneyland Hotel to shake hands with the couple. "We figured that was the best way to handle all the whispering. When the people saw Happy and the governor, they could tell she was a pleasant suburban type. It cooled that home-wrecker jazz. When Happy traveled with the governor, she had a subtle restraining effect on the press. She was pregnant, and it showed, and no one had the nerve to ask any bad-mouth questions. In fact, the Goldwater people told their troops not to discuss it, publicly or privately. Everyone was thinking that if the baby came before the primary [June 2, 1964], it would hurt the governor by reminding everyone about the divorce and remarriage. It could mean the difference in a close one."

Until the May 15 Oregon primary the Goldwater campaign was sailing along in California. But after Rockefeller's surprise victory in Oregon, "Battling Nelson" surged forward in the California polls, and the Goldwater professionals felt they had been misled into dismissing Oregon as an insignificant primary.

Goldwater launched a shakeup in his California campaign to head off Rockefeller's sudden momentum. He summoned consultants from Washington and downgraded his California handlers, chiefly the Baus and Ross political public-relations agency. Baus and Ross were completely humiliated when Goldwater's financial chairman, Henry Salvatori, started to double-check even their minor expenses for lunches and entertainment.

"I've never seen a man as mad as Barry Goldwater," Herb Baus recalled. "He acted like an enraged bull. I tell you he was so scary that I had second thoughts, right there, about a man with his temper sitting alone in a room next to that red button." (In 1966 Baus and Ross, normally a Republican agency, were to handle Governor Brown's campaign against Reagan.)

"Oregon was a real breakthrough for us," said Spencer. "Until then we were just waiting around for something to shake loose. Now Rockefeller had momentum and the Goldwater people were shaken by the extremist issue. Now, *I* don't think Barry is an extremist. But let's face it, a lot of people were worried about that and we had to go with it. So we knew our only chance was to prove that Barry was outside the mainstream— whatever the hell that is.

"All the extremist talk was making Barry defensive and he toned down a lot on television. Actually, that isn't his best medium. His printed statements *read* well— they are punchy and pithy. Goldwater should have gone more for the printed word. On TV he looks good— but the words come out wrong somehow. And when he got scared, he got bland. In print, his ideas are oversimplified but dramatic. But what the hell, a campaign is built on oversimplification."

To neutralize Rockefeller's charge of political extremism, the Goldwater camp tried to weed out Birchers and their sympathizers, but it became an impossible task. A March 19, 1964, Goldwater dinner in the Los Angeles Sports Arena revealed the senator's problem: the committee of sponsors included known members of the Society along with other Far Right groups like the "Liberty Amendment Committee," which wanted to repeal the income tax; the "Network of Patriotic Letter Writers," which circulated a map purporting to show that Irish and Mongolian troops would police the

United States under a World Government plan, and
Billy James Hargis' "Christian Crusade," which believes, among other things, that most newspapers "are
actively promoting the Communist line." Ronald Reagan, as co-chairman of the California Citizens for Goldwater, and Henry Salvatori, the chief Goldwater fund-
raiser, also attended. So did Loyd Wright, an unsuccess-
ful challenger to Tom Kuchel in the 1962 GOP senatorial
primary (Reagan had served as Wright's campaign
chairman). Wright declared in 1961: "I would give notice
to Russia to get out of the enslaved Baltic nations within
a certain time. If they didn't get out, I would commence
shooting." Wright proclaimed his belief in preventive
war: "We don't have to blow up the whole city of Moscow. But if we do, that's too bad" (Los Angeles *Times*,
December 15, 1961). He also said of the Birch Society
(Los Angeles *Times*, January 6, 1962): "I wish we had
10,000—perhaps 10 million—more of the kind of men I
know are in this Society."

Although Goldwater's campaign in California
swarmed with Birchers, California Republicans resented Rockefeller's charge that Goldwater was "outside the mainstream of the Republican party." The New
York governor's staff prepared a television documentary
to back up its claims of right-wing radicalism in California—but shelved it after weeks of indecision. The subject was too emotional and involved because of the
complex web of relationships between California's conservatives and hard-line rightists. The Rockefeller advisers concluded that the documentary was vulnerable
because there was no clear-cut line differentiating the

respectables from the wild men. This tore a hole in Rockefeller's California campaign, and his supporters had no real answer when Goldwater challenged them to provide a definition of extremism. They could not answer without hurting respectable conservatives who backed Goldwater in 1964 but who were allied with liberals and moderates in other Republican causes. Besides, the Goldwater campaign was salted with enough respectable California names, like former U.S. Senator William F. Knowland, to obviate the extremist accusation.

What Rockefeller failed to realize at the outset of the primary was the heavy inroads the Right had made toward acquiring respectability in California. Since 1962 the Birch Society had exploited the liberal-moderate weariness in California, where it now has an estimated 10,000 members, more than in any other state. The Society is especially strong in Southern California, where it exerts a heavy influence on Republican volunteer groups. Its "Support Your Local Police" campaign has attracted hundreds of police, many of whom have set up Birch cells in police departments throughout California. The Society also attracted a number of wealthy angels, including the late D. B. Lewis, president of Dr. Ross Dog Food Company, who left the Society $1,000,000 in his will.

An important shift in emphasis within the Society was engineered by former Congressman John Rousselot, whose affiliation with the Birchers had much to do with his defeat in 1962. After that defeat he turned up on the Society's payroll as Western regional vice-president and

later as national public-relations director. Rousselot
(who resigned as an employee of the Society in 1966)
moved the Birchers away from exotic concerns—like the
Right's obsession with Communist plots to confine patriots in mental asylums. Under his direction the Birch
Society became as familiar as the Chamber of Com-
merce. Birchers entered floats in parades and put up information booths at county fairs; they established book-
stores, rang doorbells, passed petitions, attended school
meetings and marched to the polls with military precision. In solid conservative areas, they registered turn-
outs of more than 90 per cent, and their workers were so
dedicated that they waited in line an hour before the
polls opened to show their strength.

Far from a ragtag mob, the Birchers in California are
articulate, well financed and effective. They have
learned how to gear into conventional politics and they
take orders without dissent. In contrast to the Left's
hairy and unwashed legions, the Birch Society presents
a well-scrubbed and well-dressed image in California;
they appear to be the epitome of suburban, solid
citizens.

By 1964 the Society had come a long way since Attorney General Stanley Mosk dismissed it in a 1961 report: "The cadre of the John Birch Society seems to be
formed primarily of wealthy businessmen, retired military officers and little old ladies in tennis shoes. They are
bound together by an obsessive fear of 'communism,' a
word which they define to include any ideas differing
from their own, even though these ideas may differ even
more markedly with the ideas of Marx, Engels, Lenin

and Khrushchev. In response to this fear, they are willing to give up a large measure of the freedoms guaranteed them by the United States Constitution in favor of accepting the dictates of their 'founder.' They seek, by fair means or foul, to force the rest of us to follow their example. They are pathetic."

In his four years on the Society's payroll, Rousselot nudged the overt racists and anti-Semites into the background and emphasized the Society's folksy, good-neighbor image. Despite its conspiratorial ways, secret membership and links with paramilitary groups, the Society presented a warm and cheery image, and Rousselot tried to segregate California Birchers from obvious hatemongers like Gerald L. K. Smith's Christian Nationalist Crusade and the American Nazi Party. But despite the changes taking place within the John Birch Society, the extremist charges were hurting Goldwater.

In the final days the polls showed Rockefeller had pulled even and that 30 per cent were still undecided. The huge number of undecideds encouraged Rockefeller because the Goldwater voters were true believers and supposedly identifiable in the polls. (But it became apparent later that many Goldwater supporters were worried about the extremist charges and misled the pollsters about their true choice.) In the last rounds Rockefeller campaigned confidently and energetically like a man smelling victory after an uphill fight. On the other hand, Goldwater acted like a man beset by invisible demons. Even when the polls showed he was ahead, he couldn't feign optimism. He didn't fear Rockefeller but he was haunted by the specter of someone else de-

railing him. If he couldn't nail down California, where
he had given hundreds of speeches for years, he couldn't
win the nomination. His brain trust feared that Nixon
would surface at the convention when the others were
too exhausted to resist—and walk off with the nomination. Goldwater was afflicted with a vague fear that the
weight of history would bear him down; somehow the
"liberal establishment" always found a way to defeat the
conservatives. It was hard for him to believe that liberal
and moderate Republicans were as weak and disunited
as they seemed.

Campaigning without regard for amenities, Goldwater referred to President Johnson and Defense Secretary McNamara in crude terms: "Light Bulb Johnson—
he's turning off the lights in the White House and we'll
turn him off in November. And Yo-Yo McNamara, we'll
get him back to making Edsels." His slangy and militant
conservatism, cutting through ceremonial ambiguities,
appealed to a new generation of middle-class rebels.
They held no traumatic memories of the Depression,
and the social reforms of the New Deal seemed anachronistic and irrelevant: they flocked to the Goldwater
cause. By Primary Day, Goldwater had 12,000 volunteers
in the field, scouring every major precinct in California. He had more amateur help than he could use—
while Rockefeller's volunteers campaigned apologeti-
cally, explaining that they preferred someone else and
simply wanted to stop Goldwater.

Then Rockefeller lost his momentum in the final days.
Richard Nixon, detecting a Rockefeller surge, reasoned
that a *meager* Rockefeller victory would kill off Gold-

water but could hardly be considered a mandate for
Rockefeller. Because an inconclusive Rockefeller victory would open the convention to a dark horse, Nixon
passed the word to his California backers: ease up on
Rockefeller. Until then, they had been working quietly
to stop Goldwater. "Those sonsabitches on the Nixon
team always operated with two sets of signals," Spencer
fumed. "That's why nobody trusts them in California."

Then Mrs. Rockefeller gave birth, and the governor
left immediately for New York. He interrupted his campaign at the crucial point and, more important, reminded the undecided voters about the double divorce
that preceded his remarriage. Meanwhile, Goldwater
splurged on newspaper advertisements and television in
the last week. Ronald Reagan appeared on TV to defend
Goldwater's civil-rights record. "Is this man a bigot?" he
asked, his voice quavering with indignation. Rockefeller returned the day before the election to make a final
air tour of California, but it was too late. Goldwater won
by only 58,000 votes in a turnout of more than 2 million.

For the first time since the Thirties, the Right was no
longer the minority faction in California's Republican
party. For decades it had been split into jealous little
factions, traveling a querulous ideological circuit, carp-
ing about the United Nations and Earl Warren. Now,
because of incredible luck and the opposition's weakness, the Right had taken a giant stride in California.
The primary showed the conservatives' strength; the
general election was to demonstrate that an actor with
the right (rather than Right) image could win.

6

"Everybody Likes Murph"

It took an old song-and-dance man, George Murphy, to prove that a Hollywood background isn't necessarily fatal in California politics. "Sure," he told crowds, "I was an actor, and a good one. I looked at a lot of my old pictures on TV, and you know what? I always played the Good Guy. I think we have had enough bad actors in politics. It's time we had a good one."

Hollywood and politics had carried on a hot-and-cold romance for years. The professionals liked celebrities because they drew crowds and raised money, but they were apprehensive about giving them more than a window-dressing role. "I guess the public will forgive an actor anything as long as he doesn't ask to be taken seriously," speculated Charlton Heston, president of the Screen Actors Guild. "The actor is like the court jester. He can pelt the King with fruit or even sit in his lap. He can get away with it—as long as he doesn't try to be King."

Since the Thirties, when Upton Sinclair won the Democratic nomination for governor, Hollywood has been heavily involved in politics. To defeat Sinclair and his End Poverty in California (EPIC) campaign, conservative movie producers banded together to make propaganda films urging Sinclair's defeat. They imported hoboes who frightened audiences by muttering into microphones that they were hired by Sinclair to invade California. During the Depression, when Sinclair had great appeal in California, Hollywood tried to fight the general discontent by producing light escapist films that proclaimed prosperity was just around the corner. In World War II the movies intensified their propagandizing with scores of anti-Axis films (many of them with racist overtones about "Krauts" and "slant-eyed monkeys"). Meanwhile, celebrities discovered that politics was an important showcase. The Democratic party, especially, leaned heavily on entertainers, and such glittering name personalities as Frank Sinatra, Paul Newman, Gregory Peck, Kirk Douglas, Danny Kaye and Jack Lemmon have supported the party. The Republicans had their celebrities—John Wayne, Cesar Romero, Walter Brennan and Irene Dunne—but the Democrats obviously possessed the most luminous names. "Who do they get at their rallies?" asked Pat Brown in 1962. "Roy Rogers and Dale Evans? They can't match us in stars." But when the rallies were over, the politicians held the celebrities at arm's length.

After Murphy won in 1964 the freeze was over. Shirley Temple, Steve Allen, Robert Vaughn, Chuck Conners, Wendell Corey and Gary Merrill had become heavily involved in politics as candidates and speechmakers. When such actors won acceptance in the tight little world of politics, politicians realized that a good actor can make a superb candidate, for a good candidate must know how to play to an audience. More important, an actor often is successful because he has a unique, or unforgettable, face, in contrast to the sameness that afflicts most public men. An actor who becomes a star is a proven crowd-getter, whose success in selling tickets is based, at least partly, on his ability to attract and hold audiences. Because of what happened in 1964, it is hard to understand why politics and show business did not legitimize their romance a lot earlier.

While Barry Goldwater lost California by 1,300,000 votes, Murphy was braving the Democratic tide. He won by more than 200,000 votes in his first race, thus encouraging Republicans who wanted to back Ronald Reagan for governor.

In the tense year of 1964—when California was distracted by Goldwaterism, a bitter fight over fair housing and an acrimonious Democratic primary— Murphy acted like a benign Irish uncle and gave California a breathing spell. He ran as a unity candidate, devoid of labels, and reminded the electorate that, even in 1964, politics could be fun. He passed out Irish shamrock campaign buttons; his supporters proclaimed, "Everybody likes Murph"—and good ol' Murph liked everyone right back.

The chief architect of Murphy's victory was Robert Finch, a brilliant attorney who managed Nixon's 1960 campaign for the Presidency. After Kennedy defeated Nixon by an eyelash in 1960, Pierre Salinger, who was then press secretary to Kennedy, derided Finch and his staff as amateurs. Finch said nothing and bided his time. Although everyone else had written off the Murphy candidacy, Finch felt the Democratic feuds were bound to hurt Salinger.

"Pierre will try to drive Murph into Goldwater's arms," Finch reflected at the start of the campaign. "But we're not going to let them fossilize George. He'll run a Good Guy campaign, appealing to unhappy Democrats as well as Republicans. Salinger cannot be as strong as the polls indicate because you cannot measure the resentment against Salinger. We'll hit him over the head with the carpetbagger issue."

Salinger was doomed, chiefly because of his illusion that the Kennedy magic could be transferred to his unmagical person. The manner of his entry clouded the election from the start. Salinger, a legal resident of Virginia, resigned as White House press secretary and flew to California in the wee hours to file for office just before the deadline. Meanwhile, Robert Kennedy, another resident of Virginia, filed for the U. S. Senate in New York. But Salinger is not Kennedy, and California is not New York. Californians, Democrats as well as Republicans, were outraged by Salinger's abrupt entrance into the primary and the Byzantine manipulations that preceded and followed it.

Governor Brown, who chose to exert leadership and lived to regret it, already had indicated his choice in the primary: State Controller Alan Cranston, a cerebral and

colorless liberal. The primary had already been tainted
because Cranston and Salinger were contesting a seat
held by another Democrat, Clair Engle, who was dying
of a brain tumor. When Governor Brown invited other
Democrats to enter the primary, he earned the unremitting enmity of Engle's friends and family. In the midst of
this bitterness, Attorney General Stanley Mosk was
forced out of the contest. Mosk, who is Jewish, was
popular with California's influential Jewish community
but decided to stay out of the race after a series of
threats and promises. Later, Governor Brown appointed
him to the State Supreme Court, touching off more
speculation about back-stage maneuvering.

When Salinger abruptly decided to challenge Cranston, you could almost hear the wheels revolving within
wheels. Salinger was Assembly Speaker Jesse Unruh's
means of combating his Democratic rivals, Brown and
Cranston. Overnight, Salinger acquired a full-fledged
campaign staff and a sizable campaign fund, which
fueled speculation that he was part of a cabal to set up a
Kennedy bloc in the Senate. At the end of a vitriolic
primary, voters got a Salinger mailer: a black-bordered
picture of President Kennedy and a plea to support candidates "in the tradition of our martyred President."
This tactic, which enraged Cranston, helped Salinger
defeat the controller by 140,000 votes.

There was more intrigue to come. After the primary,
Senator Engle died and Governor Brown appointed
Salinger, who was not eligible to vote for himself, to the
unexpired term. This touched off another round of indignation over a back-door appointment for a man who

was not a legal resident of California. Governor Brown, figuring the tumult would end when Salinger beat Murphy in November, tried to explain why he appointed a man whom he had described in the primary as being "a political rookie." "I meant rookie of the year," said Brown.

Meanwhile, Murphy waltzed through his primary, encouraged by the sounds of wreckage in the Democratic contest. There was more dirty laundry to come. The word leaked out that, despite their fight, Cranston and Salinger had worked out a cozy and unprecedented agreement to share at least part of their campaign debt. This made it convenient for the principals but imposed an improper burden on the Democratic party. Governor Brown, who was already humiliated by Cranston's defeat, had to swallow hard again. Yes, he had heard something about the agreement, he conceded, and by gosh, it wouldn't happen *again*. The more attention the Democratic primary got, the worse it smelled.

The early polls showed that either Salinger or Cranston could defeat Murphy, who got the nomination almost by default. The logical choices would have been Mayor George Christopher of San Francisco or Assemblyman Joseph Shell, but they read the polls too, and decided to wait out the Goldwater storm. Why not give a meaningless nomination to Murphy? It would be a fitting honor for an aging and amiable figure who had labored for twenty-five years in Republican activities and once served as state chairman.

Although nobody else did, Murphy took his candidacy seriously. He resented the cracks about "the *Late*

Show candidate" but laughed them off. He joked about Salinger's appearance: "Why, he doesn't even *look* like a senator," exclaimed Murphy, ruddy cheeks glowing, blue eyes twinkling under a silvery mane of senatorial hair. "A lot of Cranston Democrats are still mad at Salinger over the way he sneaked into this thing—and I'm not going to let 'em forget it. I don't expect 'em to vote for me but I don't see how they can work for Salinger after the things he and Cranston said about each other. . . .

"Salinger is the only guy who brings his own smog when he comes to Los Angeles. I guess he left the White House because he didn't like getting picked up by the ears . . ." The one-liners went over big with audiences tired of polemics and platitudes.

Murphy dodged substantive issues throughout the campaign. As a "unity candidate" he professed to see "no real difference" between Goldwater and Rockefeller: "If you put their beliefs side by side, you'll see they are pretty close." He was equally euphemistic about the Birch Society: "I don't know anything about them or Robert Welch. I started reading his book and, after getting through twenty pages, I threw it away. If they want to support me as individuals, that's okay with me." He skipped past the Goldwater embrace. "*You* have a great leader in Barry Goldwater," he assured a group of conservatives, who noticed that Murphy didn't use "*we.*" Murphy refused to take a position on fair housing, while Salinger favored it and lost support as a result.

Murphy's amiable non-campaign obscured the fact that he was a conservative, a man who occasionally complained that his career had suffered in an industry dominated by liberals. But it was a conservative, the late M-G-M boss Louis B. Mayer, who got Murphy started in politics. Mayer, who dallied in Republican affairs, liked Murphy's militant anticommunism, especially his activities on behalf of the House Committee on Un-American Activities. Mayer dispatched Murphy as Hollywood's "ambassador of goodwill" to B'nai B'rith and Knights of Columbus luncheons to dispel the idea that the movies were crawling with Reds.

After Mayer died, Murphy's career declined. Then he got a scare when doctors discovered and removed a cancerous node from his throat. Brooding and unhappy, he stayed at home. "That was the year the phone stopped ringing," he recalled, "and the bank account went all the way down." A California millionaire, Patrick Frawley, Jr., hired Murphy as director and vice-president for public relations at Technicolor, Inc., part of Frawley's corporate complex, which includes Schick Electric and Eversharp, Inc.

Frawley is an American primitive who is also a genius at business and an impulsive plunger in right-wing politics. He backed the "Christian Anti-Communism Crusade," promoted by a one-time Australian physician, Dr. Fred Schwarz, and induced Murphy to participate. But Murphy got an inside look at Dr. Schwarz' operation and backed off: "Let's just say we had a disagreement about fund-raising and leave it at that."

Meanwhile, there were rumors that California's Right was out to ruin Tom Kuchel's career in the U. S. Senate. Eventually, a curious pamphlet showed up, purporting that Kuchel had been arrested with another man for drunken driving in 1950 and that one of the police officers had noticed signs of an "immoral act." Five men were arrested on charges of criminal libel—and one of them was on Frawley's payroll. John Fergus, who had been hired as a sales representative for the Schick division, pleaded no contest and paid a $500 fine. Frawley appeared in court and swore that he had no knowledge of the false circular. He also testified that he hired Fergus in a public-relations capacity after hearing of his "patriotic reputation." Frawley, who insisted he was surprised and embarrassed by Fergus, fired him. But the incident deepened the Republican split; Kuchel demanded that Murphy repudiate the Far Right and Murphy refused. Kuchel then refused to endorse Murphy. A number of Technicolor executives resigned because of political differences with Frawley, who had stocked the Technicolor offices with Murphy's campaign literature. Murphy, who had been hired by Frawley when he needed a job badly, remained at Technicolor, but he too was embarrassed by the Fergus incident. "I really don't see much of Pat Frawley," he said during the campaign. "I'm over at Technicolor and Frawley is busy making razor blades."

Throughout his career, Murphy had relied on his ingratiating ways to align himself with achievers, Mayer at M-G-M, then Frawley. But at age sixty-two, when he entered the Senate race, he was haunted by a sense of unfulfillment. Everyone liked him but no one took him seriously. He wanted to shuck off his lightweight, song-and-dance image. Like Salinger, he had hovered around the periphery of power and seemed to have acquired a taste for it while holding other men's coats. Now he wanted to be his own man, and the polls showed he had a chance to win if he could keep Salinger on the defensive.

But Murphy and his involvement with Frawley were not the issue in 1964; Salinger was. He had irritated the voters by overemphasizing his relationship with President Kennedy, and the use of Kennedy-style rhetoric sounded contrived when uttered by the pudgy, dark-browed candidate. Unlike Murphy, who reveled in the public eye, Salinger squirmed in his new role as a campaigner. He fidgeted with crowds and gave up smoking cigars in public for the duration of the campaign. But it did not help; the September polls showed that Murphy had gained eight points. And Salinger panicked: he agreed to debate Murphy on television.

Salinger reasoned that, having worked in Washington, he was more knowledgeable about government and that a debate on television would expose Murphy's deficiencies. But he ignored Murphy's own expertise on television and his own problems in the medium. Although Salinger was the incumbent, he looked like a challenger, and an uneasy one at best. On the other hand, Murphy was an old hand at masking his anxiety in public. He radiated confidence and amiability before the cameras, remembering to address himself to the audience (an estimated 3.5 million Californians watched the October 5, 1964, debate on TV), while Salinger tried to score debaters' points. The more he tried to trip up Murphy, the more the audience sympathized with the older man. At the end the confrontation took on a melodramatic aspect. Would the beetle-browed villain entrap good ol' Murph? Could Murphy sidestep Salinger's bull-like rushes for the full sixty minutes? In his haste to deflate Murphy, Salinger looked as irritable and mean as "the heavy" in an old gangster film while Murphy, twinkling and beaming without pause, exuded sincerity and courtliness. Salinger disturbed the audience, and Murphy soothed it.

On the weekend before the debate Murphy watched Salinger on a television panel and realized he had a patsy. "He's glib and he's smart," said Murphy. "But Pierre is too forceful. Every time he raises his voice, he looks like he's covering up a lack of information. I don't think he will be too tough. Besides, he looks bad on the tube. Sly and disrespectful.

"I'm not cramming new facts. I'm going to hit the points I've made all through the campaign. The over-all approach, not the specific points, will decide the debate. I'm going for the undecideds. They are the ones who care what a fella *looks* like. I have to paint a positive picture. If the undecideds feel a fella is on the level, that's a plus; that he knows a lot, that's a plus; that he's experienced, that's a plus; that the other guy hasn't been around too long, that's a plus for Murph. If I can overcome the song-and-dance image, I'll be in good shape."

The debate turned out as Murphy expected. When the camera focused on the two men together, the image was irrevocably set: Murphy looked like a senator and Salinger like a loser. The rest was forgettable; the sly digs and the counterthrusts seemed to cancel out each other. Both men stuck to generalities and, aside from the physical images, there was hardly anything that remained in the audience's consciousness. When Salinger tried to break through with a disconcerting question, he looked like an awkward lunger. Murphy and Finch had anticipated his thrusts anyway. When Pierre brought up Goldwater, Murphy suggested, "Why don't you go to Arizona and run against him?" And when he replied to Salinger's predictable question about the "Christian Anti-Communism Crusade," Murphy looked like a cat who had swallowed a delicious pigeon. "You will be glad to know," he beamed, "that one of our outstanding senators was the keynote speaker: Senator Thomas Dodd from Connecticut, who is a good friend of mine and who, incidentally, rode to Atlantic City with the President in a place of honor on the airplane."

At the end of the debate Salinger looked like a man who had just seen a grisly accident on the freeway. "I guess this shows the futility of trying to come to grips with anyone as slippery as my opponent," he groused. Murphy emerged in triumph as if he had just won the Academy Award. Four weeks later, when he defeated Salinger, Governor Brown observed, "California is a very funny state. Californians don't vote parties, they vote men." And now that Murphy had broken the barrier against actors, Ronald Reagan could emerge in big-time politics.

7

Unfinished Business

After he lost the 1964 Presidential election by 15 million votes, Barry Goldwater paid tribute to his heir presumptive. "I have always looked on Ronald Reagan as one of the leaders of the conservative movement in this country," the Arizona senator said. "And I would say that, if he continues in his successful political career, I don't think you could deny that he would be the leader. And I would very, very gladly serve with him, under him or alongside of him."

Two weeks later, the first Reagan-for-President unit was formed in Owosso, Michigan, as the first overt step in Reagan's plan to inherit and expand Goldwater's 27 million. In ordinary times it would have seemed incredible that a man who had delivered a half-hour speech on national TV on behalf of a defeated candidate could go as fast and as far as Reagan. But 1964 was no ordinary year in American history. The events of that watershed year made it possible for Reagan to become a candidate in 1966; Reagan, the persuasive salesman, would replace Barry, the tough-talking sheriff.

During the 1964 campaign Reagan excited the crowds as much as Goldwater. He cemented his hold on conservatives by working as co-chairman of California Citizens for Goldwater. He had known the senator for years, having met Goldwater while visiting in Phoenix. Goldwater spoke glowingly of Reagan, and the actor often reminded listeners that Goldwater was not defeated—"The opposition simply created a distorted image and defeated that."

The day after the Johnson landslide, Reagan in effect launched his unannounced campaign for governor by declaring at a press conference that conservative Republicanism now was "the mainstream" of the party. A week later he told Los Angeles County's rightward-bound Young Republicans: "We don't intend to turn the Republican party over to the traitors in the battle just ended. . . . The conservative philosophy was not repudiated. We will have no more of those candidates who are pledged to the same Socialist goals of our opposition and who seek our support. If after the California Presidential primary our opponents had then joined Barry Goldwater at the national convention and pledged their support, we could very well be celebrating a complete victory tonight."

After the tumultuous reaction to Reagan's Goldwater speech, the Democrats had fully expected that Reagan would win the Republican nomination for governor. Pat Brown figured a patsy like Reagan would get him off the hook. And so the campaign, which could have been a vital dialogue between liberal and conservative, became a cosmetic contest from the start.

The Democrats hoped to ignore questions about their eight-year stewardship by waging a Good Guy–Bad Guy campaign. Although California had tired of Pat Brown, the party hierarchy had discouraged new leaders. After only eight years in office the Democrats had become remarkably fat in the soul. The party no longer was a conduit for progressive ideas but a franchise for self-seekers, a tool for whoever was crafty or tough enough to grasp and wield power.

Assuming that they could count on Republican aberrations to help them stay in power indefinitely, the Democrats hoped to use Reagan's inexperience and his impetuous right-wing statements to scare California into giving Brown a third term. Reagan started his candidacy with considerable disadvantages. He had not even bothered to change his registration until 1962, although he had supported Republicans since 1952. "I didn't desert my party," he explained. "It deserted me. I looked up FDR's old platform, and I discovered that it called for a restoration of states' rights and a reduction in the national budget. You know what? I'm still for that. And wasn't it Churchill who said he'd rather change his party for principles than his principles for his party?" But despite his ingenuous ways, Reagan was distrusted by many conservatives and resented by politicians in both parties. If this newcomer could win, they reasoned, anybody with stage presence and money could, and that would end their cozy game. As Reagan emerged, other politicians began to seem dowdy and anachronistic, as if they had aged overnight.

The Democrats decided they had made a mistake in

1964 by not taking George Murphy seriously until it was too late. Now they determined to get Reagan early, and a team of researchers combed through the minutiae of his public and private life. They compiled a heavy dossier of impolitic public statements that assumed encyclopedic proportions months before his nomination. By overreacting to their mistakes of 1964, the Democrats exposed their cynicism and ideological bankruptcy; the leadership had nothing to offer except a bogeyman campaign, and the old theory of spend and elect seemed as dated as a Thirties movie. In less troubled times Pat Brown's pragmatic liberalism suited California, but in 1966 the voters wanted to know why a state so favored in economic and natural bounty was roiled with racial tension, crime and high taxes. The liberals not only lacked answers, they no longer even asked the questions. They were too busy defending the status quo. To the intellectuals they offered platitudes; to minorities they proclaimed the other guy was worse; to union members they recalled battles won thirty years ago. They had their story and they were stuck with it: You never had it so good, and don't let that actor take it away.

But California was in deep trouble behind its golden façade of prosperity, having paid a numbing price in the numbers game known as progress. Since World War II the population had doubled and the headaches had increased tenfold: state spending up 1,552 per cent, taxes up 813 per cent, state employees up 328 per cent. Per capita taxes were only $47.51 in 1948 but soared to $157.36 in 1966.

Many newcomers were poor, unskilled and barely literate, having migrated to California to get jobs in industry only to find their visions shattered by a technological revolution that produced industries dependent on sophisticated computers and skilled manpower. Nevertheless the migration continued, the greatest westward movement since the Gold Rush. From 1950 to 1960 nearly 1,500,000 Negroes left the Old South, and almost one-fourth of them ended their journey in California. Since Pearl Harbor the Negro population in Los Angeles County had increased nearly tenfold, to more than 650,000. The muscle-power jobs that lured them to California faded away with automation, and the financial burdens created by this migration descended on California like a leaden albatross. It costs more than three-quarters of a billion dollars each year for aid to California's indigent and orphaned children, the blind, mentally ill and retarded and physically disabled. For each new family arriving in California the state must pay more than $13,000 a year for classrooms, fire and police protection, sewers and other public health facilities. (An untold number of families arriving in California get a free tax ride: they leave the state after a year without paying state income tax because California has no withholding system and no means of finding evaders.)

Meanwhile, California enjoys a mixed blessing in the federal spending which fueled the postwar migration. It is the number one state in federal employment, and the federal payroll in California, with a half-million employees, is the largest in the nation. Defense and aerospace industries account for nearly 40 per cent of all

manufacturing employment, creating six out of every
ten new jobs. California gets nearly one out of every five
federal dollars spent on defense and aerospace. A state
so heavily dependent on the whims of a remote federal
establishment obviously is in trouble if the government
abruptly changes course. A slowdown in federal spending could be disastrous to California's heavily dependent economic base. But, for some Californians, economic disaster is a daily reality.

The Depression never ended in the Negro community
of Watts, one of many small neighborhoods in Los
Angeles' 50-square-mile Black Belt. Watts is neither a
legal nor a political entity. Although it is less than one-
tenth of the ghetto's area, it is a port of entry for Southern Negroes in south-central Los Angeles. In a glittering
city, where squalor is hidden as subtly as the cemeteries,
Watts is the nucleus of Negro frustration. About one-
third of the young men in Watts are unemployed. Annual income for the black family in Watts is approximately half that of the white family in the San Fernando
Valley, the chief suburb of Los Angeles. The school
dropout rate in Watts is 2.5 times higher than among
whites; one-third of Watts' schoolchildren come from
broken homes; one-fourth are illegitimate; more than
half of the families are on relief of some kind. In a city
where buildings constantly are torn down in pursuit of
the new and the chic, 87 per cent of the homes in the
ghetto predate 1939; one-fifth of the homes are officially
classified as deteriorated or dilapidated.

Apologists for Los Angeles contend that its Black Belt
is cleaner, less crowded and more attractive than older

ghettos in New York and Chicago. But in a relatively
young city, Watts is more than a painful embarrassment; it is a disgraceful reminder of the widening gap
between Los Angeles' two worlds. To the ghetto, there is
special irony in the knowledge that, until Watts exploded on August 11, 1965, thousands of whites drove by
it on the Harbor Freeway and did not know of its existence. Miles of terraced freeway embankments obscure
the sun-stricken, flat and dusty streets of Watts, and no
whites, except for police, social workers and teachers,
stopped there. Before the uprising Watts was a place
you passed at 65 miles per hour on your way to work.

The problems that festered in Watts were intensified
by tension between police and Negroes; years of cold
war that occasionally led to bloodshed were usually
ignored by Los Angeles' metropolitan newspapers. The
late William H. Parker, a hard-nosed and puritanical
police chief, insisted on rigid enforcement of the law,
and he made no allowances for the painful transition
Negroes had to make from South to West, from rural to
urban living. Many Southern Negroes knew that police
back home were indifferent to black crime as long as it
was confined to Negro neighborhoods. But Los Angeles'
police had deprived them of the Saturday night freedom
they enjoyed back home. The Negroes in Watts lacked
the diversions permitted them as an escape valve in
other cities. The children of Watts had no movie house,
bowling alley or skating rink, and they felt life was pass-
ing them by, as disinterestedly as the cars on the freeway. Police cars patrolled the Black Belt like an army of
occupation, and few Negroes in Watts have escaped

humiliating encounters with police. But City Hall gave only perfunctory attention to complaints of police brutality.

As tensions increased, the civil-rights leadership tried to meet with Police Chief Parker, but he brusquely rejected their entreaties. Civil rights had always been a middle-class movement in California, and the police chief sarcastically reminded them that they were leaders without followers in the ghetto. In a sense the chief was right: Los Angeles' civil-rights leaders were Negroes who, having made it in white society, wanted to live in integrated neighborhoods and leave Watts to the poor. In the anxious year of 1964 one civil-rights leader—Dr. H. Hartford Brookins, pastor of Los Angeles' First African-Methodist Episcopal Church—spoke with prophetic insight:

> The Negroes here feel a sense of urgency from the impact of recent events, even before the riots in Harlem. This is a young city, and the seeds of unrest are not as apparent here. Los Angeles is not as rigid, and the Negro population is not concentrated quite so dramatically in blocks or belts, but it is coming. There is danger, great danger, because the power structure is not taking the Negroes here seriously. There are lines of communication, but no one sees sufficient reason to use them. If and when the Rumford Fair Housing Act is repealed, it will raise the stock of extremist Negro groups. They have been working all along, telling our people that they shouldn't expect anything anyway from whites.

In 1964 California held its great debate on fair housing. Nothing on the California ballot had so exacerbated emotions as the fight over Proposition 14, a proposed amendment to the State Constitution repealing significant portions of the Rumford Housing Act and two earlier civil-rights statutes. The amendment also barred the Legislature from enacting new antidiscrimination measures in housing without submitting them first to a costly and uncertain vote of the people.

The 40,000-member California Real Estate Association, which has a long history of promoting racial separatism, led the campaign for 14. In 1943 the association opposed the return of Japanese-Americans to the West Coast; in 1948, after the U. S. Supreme Court struck down restrictive covenants, the association supported a campaign to amend the U. S. Constitution to permit such covenants. The CREA wanted to amend the California Constitution so the Legislature could not tamper with segregated housing. In 1963 the Democratic-dominated Legislature passed the Rumford Housing Act, and the realtors saw their chance to arouse the public. Californians felt the Rumford Act was an unwarranted intrusion in their private lives, although its wording was so vague and innocuous that anyone who really wanted to discriminate could easily do so. Confusion about the new law, coupled with anxiety over riots in the East, assured the realtors of success.

Although the vote on Proposition 14 has been invalidated by the California and the U. S. Supreme Court, the ill will fostered by the campaign shredded the moderate-progressive coalition in California, encouraged the racists, estranged the union leadership from

the rank-and-file, ministers from congregations and the
Democratic party from its traditional allies. The atmosphere was already overheated when Governor Brown
declared that:

> The vast and impersonal California Real Estate
> Association, using our initiative and referendum
> process, set about to wipe the law off the books
> and, with it, many civil-rights laws of long stand-
> ing. Immediately, the shock troops of bigotry
> moved in behind the real estate association: the
> White Citizens Council, the John Birch Society,
> the American Nazi party.
>
> Since then, there have been echoes in this state
> of another hate binge which began more than
> thirty years ago in a Munich beer hall. These
> echoes come from a minority of the angry, the
> frustrated, the fearful. They do not represent Cali-
> fornia or its people. But what they do represent—
> the spasm reaction of hatred—does exist not only
> in California but elsewhere in our nation and in
> our world.

The governor's words inflamed the issue. White Citizens Councils sprang up in Southern California under
the slogan "White Men, Unite." The Birch Society, exploiting the issue to recruit members, distributed Proposition 14 petitions and leaflets. "The essence of freedom
is the right to discriminate," declared Nolan Frizzelle,
president of the 20,000-member California Republican
Assembly. "Discrimination means free choice. In Socialist countries they always take away this right in order to

complete their takeover." The California Young Repub-
licans also recommended passage; former YR President
Robert Gaston declared: "Negroes are not accepted be-
cause they haven't made themselves acceptable." A new
organization, calling itself the California Committee for
Home Protection, hired as consultant one William K.
Shearer, whose writings have been reprinted in the Citi-
zens Councils' publication *The Citizen* in Mississippi.
Shearer contended that the Republican party, under
Barry Goldwater, could overturn the Democrats in the
South "once the GOP kicks over the ball and chain of
integration."

California rallied around the potent argument of
"freedom." Freedom, absolute and unhindered, to do
what one pleases, to rent or to sell as one chooses. To
many homeowners and apartment owners government
is an oppressive, impersonal and impervious authority,
blindly bulldozing homes to make way for freeways and
urban renewal. Southern California, where anti-
Rumford feeling ran strongest, is the land of the small
homeowner. His home is the only constant in unending
change, an impregnable fortress to which he can retire
in isolation from his neighbors and reality. Reality in-
trudes nonetheless: there are scores of restrictions on
what a homeowner may or may not do with his property.
But the myth of absolute freedom led him to believe that
the Rumford Act took away something that he never
really possessed.

From the first, Pat Brown's cautious instincts told him
that the state was not ready for a broad social experi-
ment such as the Rumford Fair Housing Act. The State

Assembly had passed the fair housing bill and sent it to the Senate, where most observers assumed it would die. Meanwhile, civil-rights groups pressured the governor to pry the bill out of committee, and Pat Brown's advisers assured him they could work out amendments to make the bill palatable to the housing industry. To further muffle the anticipated objections, the governor's Fair Employment Practices Commission passed the word that it would enforce the law circumspectly. Although Pat Brown was never totally convinced he went along, assured that he would thus be remembered as a social innovator like his idol Earl Warren. After key amendments were worked out with lobbyists for the California Real Estate Association, the bill was passed in the final minutes before adjournment of the 1963 legislative session.

The Rumford Act is a vague, technically flawed piece of legislation that covers all publicly assisted housing and privately financed units of five or more, which means approximately one-third of all homes and apartments in California. The act does not compel property owners to rent or sell to Negroes; it simply declares that the owner may not offer property on the open market, then withdraw it solely because of racial or religious objections. The statute establishes a lengthy mediation and conciliation procedure. If all attempts at mediation fail, the FEPC can order the owner to make available the house or apartment or, if the property is no longer on the market, require the owner to pay up to $500 damages to the complainant. The owner may appeal the fine in court. Opponents predicted that Negroes would flood

the FEPC with frivolous complaints but the commission
got fewer than 200 in the first year of the Act's existence.
Whites feared their neighborhoods would be inundated,
but it was never explained how California could be
inundated by 6 per cent of the population.

The "No on 14" campaign was supported by unions,
churches, the PTA, the League of Women Voters, and
the Hollywood colony. The other side had the voters as
well as a $100,000 line of credit established by the National
Association of Real Estate Boards and the promise of
more if needed. It had an army of realtors and real estate
salesmen, covert help from the Birch Society and a 500-
man speakers' bureau. Billboards throughout the state
urged "Freedom of Choice," and millions of homeowners in the final weeks got letters soliciting their
"prayerful consideration."

In the housing fight, low-income white Democrats
left their leadership. For the blue-collar worker living in
the path of the ghetto's expansion the question of integrated housing became a fight for survival. "Don't ask
me about civil rights," a white woman told an inter-
viewer. "I don't want to talk about it. If I had a gun, I'd
kill every nigger on this block."

California passed Proposition 14 by more than two to
one. And, as predicted, it cut the ground from under the
civil-rights leadership. Although most Negroes could
not afford to leave the ghetto in any event, it was a bitter
psychological blow that strengthened those militants
who had argued that it was futile to expect fair play from
whites. The California and the U. S. Supreme Court declared the repeal amendment unconstitutional, but that

did not alter the painful realization: most whites did not
want Negroes for neighbors. Before the 1964 vote civil-
rights groups held protest demonstrations that, if nothing else, served as a nonviolent channel for the expres-
sion of grievances. After the vote on Proposition 14 even
that seemed irrelevant. Now California was headed for
racial violence that would pave the way for new political alignments.

When Watts erupted August 11, 1965, the supposedly
tough and mobile police seemed stunned and uncertain
in the first two days of violence. The rioters made a
mockery of the police, who occasionally stood by pas-
sively as the rioters burned and looted stores. Meanwhile, Police Chief Parker continued making Colonel
Blimp pronouncements on television: it was all the fault
of the courts, whose decisions hampered police; the
rioters were acting like "monkeys in the zoo"; civil-
rights leaders were "pseudo-leaders, largely demagogic,
trying to put themselves in front"; Negro leaders had
prevailed upon police not to publish statistics of Negro
crime because "it's not nice." Eventually, he said, looking pained, central Los Angeles would be 45 per cent
Negro. "How are you going to live with that?" he asked.
"Without law enforcement? If you don't have a strong
police department and law and order, God help you!" It
took five days for the National Guard to restore
order, and afterward the police chief told a television
audience, "We're on top and they are on the bottom."

Although it was obvious his police couldn't cope with
the violence, Chief Parker emerged as the only hero,
chiefly because his racist statements meshed with Cali-

fornia's growing mood of white intransigence. The
chief, who got a standing ovation at an American
Legion convention, humiliated Dr. Martin Luther King,
who flew to Los Angeles to help restore order. "I am not
going to yield," the chief told Dr. King in the mayor's
office. "I am absolutely inflexible. There is a criminal
element here, and I mean to deal with it." Dr. King, who
also was jeered in Watts, left the city a disillusioned and
defeated man. "I hate to be a bad host," the chief
crowed, "but I could not accommodate Dr. King by
resigning."

After peace was restored, Governor Brown appointed
an eight-member commission to investigate the causes
of the riot and make recommendations. John A.
McCone, an industrialist who once headed the Central
Intelligence Agency and the Atomic Energy Commission, was named chairman. He took the job at the urging
of the White House, and immediately adopted what he
called an "inventory approach" to a problem that cried
out for a broad social orientation. From the start
McCone was inhibited by what he considered the limits
of public acceptance, and the commission's 101-page
summary of its findings turned into a superficial reap-
praisal of facts already known. It made minimal recommendations but failed to sift, probe or weigh the underlying causes of tension. McCone steadfastly refused to
consider the issue of housing segregation, asserting that
this problem will take care of itself as Negroes make
themselves more acceptable through education and a
higher standard of living.

"If you try to change the basic thinking of the great

American public," Chairman McCone declared, "you are getting into an area that would take years to resolve. We wanted immediate solutions, not theories. You find segregation throughout the world—Moscow, Brazil, South Africa. We are not unique in that sense. We are unique in this country because here *we have always taken care of the Negro people*. Always. And we will continue."

The commission gave McCone what he wanted and also preserved a gentleman's agreement: the only public official criticized in the report was Lieutenant Governor Glenn M. Anderson, whom Pat Brown had been trying to dump anyway. The report concluded that Anderson, who was acting governor while Brown was vacationing in Greece, "hesitated when he should have acted." By offering up Anderson as a scapegoat, the Democrats thought they paid a small price in explaining what happened in Watts.

But it was the issue that made Reagan's victory a certainty.

8

The Cram Course

When Ronald Reagan first asked the Spencer-Roberts agency to handle his campaign, the partners stalled a while. They knew that Pat Brown was vulnerable but they were uncertain that Reagan could topple him.

Reagan met with Spencer, Roberts and Fred Haffner (their Northern California partner) in April, 1965, and they held several exploratory sessions. Bill Roberts, a beefy, balding bachelor who usually handles the conservative clients, did most of the talking at the first meeting.

"There was never any question that Ron was an exciting personality who could attract important money," said Roberts, "but we wanted to get a better idea of the man's philosophy. We told Ron flat out that we did not want to get involved in a Goldwater-type campaign, and Ron said he understood and sympathized. We made it clear that politics isn't like Hollywood; we were trained professionals and we wanted to be treated that way. A candidate cannot be a star and treat his staff like dirt. We were not an entourage, we were consultants, and we made it clear that we don't work for dogmatists or prima donnas. Ron respected us for laying our cards out, and he agreed all the way."

The men met in Reagan's home and peppered him with questions. Finally, Reagan got tired of the inquisition and blurted out, "Now, goddamit, I want to get some answers from you guys. Are you going to work for me or not?" The partners thought about it a few days and said yes. They had received a feeler from George Christopher, the former mayor of San Francisco, but the partners were not interested. "We never go into an obvious turkey situation," said Bill Roberts. "George is a nice guy, but we felt that California wanted a candidate who could excite people. How are you going to charge the voters with a guy who reminds you of Pat Brown?"

The political technicians decided that Ron not only spoke well but could quickly pick up the essentials. They started moving him around the state in a precampaign buildup and meanwhile they developed the rudiments of an organization. The original plan, paid for by "Friends of Ronald Reagan," was to give Reagan an "out-of-town tryout" for six months, and, if the act went over, to put up "important money" for a full-fledged campaign. Meanwhile, Reagan was to tell the curious that he was merely traveling around the state learning the issues.

"We moved him around a lot," said Bill Roberts, "and we kept him close to knowledgeable people so he could learn about the state. Everybody was getting curious about his chances but Ron kept saying he just wanted to see if he could unite all elements of the party. He played it very coolly."

To make certain that Reagan knew the issues, the political agency hired a team of conservative academicians at the Behavior Science Corporation (BASICO) of Los Angeles to provide Reagan with a cram course. The results of the course paid off when Reagan, who usually quoted *The Reader's Digest,* started to salt his remarks with quotations from Hillaire Belloc and Edmund Burke. The experts from BASICO compiled volumes of research on California problems—education, welfare, taxes, labor, minorities, agriculture and "morality in government"—and reduced it to neatly typed and indexed four-by-five-inch cards. The cards were contained in a notebook which Reagan kept at his side during the year-long campaign.

"We were hired to do for Reagan what the academicians did for Rockefeller," explains BASICO President Stanley Plog. "We had to get more informational input into Reagan's speeches and to provide a philosophical and historical framework for his beliefs.

"We took his philosophy and extrapolated it into concrete programs in seventeen identifiable state issues. The problem was to flesh out these programs in a way that was consistent with the candidate's basic philosophy, and we needed statistics to buttress his ideas."

The academicians accompanied Reagan on all his public tours for six months, checking the crowd reaction and trying to anticipate problems. Plog, a behavioral psychologist, alternated on the trips with Kenneth Holden, another psychologist and executive vice-president of BASICO. At times Reagan's intellectual shadows drew derisive comments from critics, who contended that Spencer and Roberts surrounded him with experts to prevent him from popping off. The men from BASICO were derided as "special agents with gun and license to kill."

"We also performed another function," says Stanley Plog. "Our presence reminded the press of the candidate's intellectual underpinnings. It was not quite so easy to dismiss Reagan as an anti-intellectual when they saw him traveling with a college professor. The working press was very hostile to Reagan, especially at first, but this feeling was mitigated somewhat by the fact that his entourage did include academicians."

To shore up Reagan's philosophical foundations, BASICO's research staff (which numbered as many as twenty-nine part-time assistants) culled the works of Edmund Burke, Alexander Hamilton, John Marshall, David Hume, John Adams, James Madison, Thomas Jefferson, Alexis de Tocqueville, Benjamin Disraeli, Abraham Lincoln, Oliver Wendell Holmes, Herbert Croly, Herbert Hoover, Robert A. Taft, William F. Buckley, Jr., Reinhold Niebuhr, Willmoore Kendall, Ortega y Gasset, Plato and Aristotle. "You should have seen those newspapermen jump when Ron first quoted Jefferson to them." Kenneth Holden laughed.

The press expected to find a glib celebrity but instead they discovered a man who had done his homework and who could more than hold his own in question-and-answer sessions. "It hurt us," said Pat Brown, "because the press expected to find a complete dummy, and when Reagan turned out to be well-briefed, they overreacted as if he were some kind of genius." The matter of his credibility as a serious candidate was Reagan's chief problem, and BASICO helped him overcome that handicap.

"We made certain that Reagan came across as a reasonable guy," said Kenneth Holden, "not as a fanatic who wanted to tear down all government. One of the first things I got Ron to do was to stop using that terrible phrase, 'totalitarian ant heap.' It just sounded too harsh. His basic speech was too negative, so we provided him with creative alternatives to combat that Far Right image with constructive proposals. We discovered the chief complaint in 1966 was the feeling that government was no longer responsive to human needs, and we wanted him to offer proposals to make government more efficient and human."

The rest of Reagan's staff felt a bit uneasy in the company of the academicians. "We had to play the heavies, the voice of dissent," said Kenneth Holden. "There is a self-reinforcing quality about campaigns, especially if the candidate is a movie celebrity, and everyone tends to echo what the candidate says. We had to provide criticism but we moved cautiously because the others were suspicious. They kept reminding us that our function was to research issues, not to formulate policy. And, of course, we approached Ron cautiously. When we prefaced a suggestion by saying that another approach might have more impact, Ron was fairly reasonable. But he made it clear that he did not want to look like a mouthpiece for someone else. That mouthpiece thing bothered him throughout the campaign because he had been doing his own research for years; he took us to his house and showed us piles of clippings in boxes, and he was pretty proud of his collection. He insisted that everything we put out reflect his approach because he did not want to have the opposition say we were putting words in his mouth."

While Reagan traveled around California, the moderates argued for months about an effective primary challenger. The obvious choice, Senator Thomas Kuchel, decided to stay out of the contest, and the only moderate left with sufficient name exposure to challenge Reagan was the experienced but uninspiring George Christopher. In competing against Christopher in the primary, Ronald Reagan got what amounted to a dress rehearsal for Pat Brown in the general election.

Both Christopher and Brown are traditional politicians who settle comfortably into the amorphous folds of the political middle. When party labels are removed, their political views are nearly identical. Both are San Franciscans and their popularity falls off sharply in Southern California. George Christopher and Pat Brown excel in the palm-pressing and back-slapping school of politics, but they are ponderously unexciting on television. Christopher matches Brown in malapropisms. "It is time to restore moral turpitude to government," the mayor told an audience, rivaling Pat Brown's classic about the floods in Northern California: "This is the greatest disaster since I was elected governor."

The other primary opposition was negligible: U.S. Attorney Laughlin Waters, a moderate hardly known outside Los Angeles, and an erratic cosmetics manufacturer, William Penn Patrick, who promised, "I'll watch *Death Valley Days* if Ronnie promises to use my pancake makeup." Months before the June primary it was obvious that Reagan was the front-runner, and the other hopefuls tried to trip him up. Former Assemblyman Joseph C. Shell, who had expected conservative backing in 1966, said Reagan failed to honor a commitment to support him for governor, and Reagan quickly denied it.

Soon Reagan became everybody's favorite target. Laughlin Waters accused Reagan at a panel discussion of "political dishonesty" for not admitting that he was a candidate. George Christopher noted that Reagan was a political switch-hitter who moved from left to right and now appeared to be heading for the middle. When the clamor escalated, the Republican state chairman, Dr. Gaylord Parkinson, lowered the volume permanently. For the first time in history, the Republican primary's traditional bloodletting was disallowed by Parkinson's invocation of the "Eleventh Commandment": "Thou shalt not speak ill of any other Republican." Parkinson threatened to cut off party funds for violators. Obviously, the edict helped the front-runner, Reagan; the others protested but could do nothing. Later, supporters of Christopher complained that Reagan's brain trust had influenced Dr. Parkinson by contributing heavily to a $33,000 fund to defray the young obstetrician's expenses. (After the campaign, the coolly professional Dr. Parkinson negotiated to handle the campaign of Governor George Romney of Michigan, but Romney's organization turned the doctor down because his price was too high: he wanted a reported minimum of $37,000 plus Romney's advertising contract in eleven Western states. Eventually, Parkinson emerged in Washington as

Richard Nixon's campaign chairman, but he resigned a few months later, citing his wife's illness.)

The drumfire within the party abated, but Reagan was still under attack. There were reports that backers of Reagan and Christopher had worked out a secret deal—to unite behind whoever had the best chance of beating Brown, on the basis of polls in December, 1965—and that Reagan's people reneged. Reagan's chief fundraiser, Henry Salvatori, came out of the shadows long enough to out-finesse the opposition. Yes, he purred, there had been a meeting, but it had been an informal get-together to consider ways to unite the party behind the nominee.

Although he maintained his calm publicly, Reagan blew his stack in private. "He couldn't understand why guys in his own party would go after him like that," said Bill Roberts. "What the hell, he figured, we're all Republicans. We're the guys in the white hats, we ought to be saving our ammunition for the bad guys. Ron really got hot when they insinuated that he didn't keep his word."

At a crucial point in the primary, Reagan finally blew up in public, and at the worst of all possible times. It happened at the March 6, 1966, convention of the Negro Republican Assembly, where Reagan appeared along with Christopher and William Penn Patrick (Laughlin Waters had dropped out of the race in January). Reagan's appearance meant nothing in terms of the meager political leverage exercised by Negroes in California's WASP-oriented Republican party. "We knew Ron wasn't going to get anywhere with Negroes," said Stu Spencer, "but he had to go anyway because it would look bad if he stayed away." Reagan fidgeted when his opponents explained why they supported the Civil Rights Act of 1964—and he bristled when Christopher cited his civil-rights record in San Francisco.

Reagan knew what to expect; he had been briefed for two days by BASICO. But his face clouded as the meeting progressed; he had characterized the Civil Rights Act as "a badly written piece of legislation" and declared he would have voted against it on technical grounds. But when a Negro delegate declared, "It grieves me when a leading Republican candidate says the Civil Rights Act is a bad piece of legislation," Reagan could not contain himself. He flung his research cards down and asked for a point of personal privilege. "I resent the implication that there is any bigotry in my nature," he shouted. "Don't anyone ever imply that I lack integrity. I will not stand still and let anyone imply that—in this or any other group." With tears in his eyes, Reagan walked out of the hall, muttering "I'll get that sonofabitch," while Christopher watched him, dumfounded.

Reagan was furious with Christopher but no one at the meeting could understand why; Christopher had discussed his own civil-rights record and had not mentioned Reagan. However, he had been needling him for weeks and Reagan, who can only hold his temper so long, was long overdue for an outburst. The Negro convention gave him his first opportunity in a direct confrontation with Christopher.

His dramatic exit cast a pall over the delegates, who talked in quiet clusters and speculated over why Reagan had gotten so angry. Kenneth Holden, who had helped brief Reagan, was shocked by the outburst. "I knew that Reagan had been doing a slow burn at Christopher and this was Ron's first chance to confront him," said Holden. "But under the circumstances, this was the worst place in the world for Ron to blow up. The press would interpret it as a walkout on the Negro delegates." Holden telephoned Reagan's home in Pacific Palisades and asked Nancy Reagan to talk to her husband. Finally Reagan came to the telephone, somewhat cooled down, and Holden pleaded with him. "Look, Ron, it really looks bad if you leave that way. The delegates didn't do anything to you; Christopher did. Right now everybody is wandering around trying to figure out what happened. Why don't you come back and have a drink with the delegates? It will ease a lot of hurt feelings." By the time Reagan returned to the hotel the press had gone; he walked into the hospitality room, chatted with the delegates and then left.

The opposition had counted on Reagan to defeat himself, and the headlines in the Sunday newspapers made the situation look dismal. Spencer and Roberts dismissed the incident in public but privately they warned Reagan that another outburst could mean the end of his career. If the opposition could prove to the electorate that he was as thin-skinned as the insiders knew he was, that would take a considerable gloss off his aura of amiability. As long as he kept calm, he appealed to the uncommitted as a dedicated "citizen-politician."

"The citizen-politician image was a great thing to fall back on," said Bill Roberts. "When something came up that Ron didn't know, all he had to do was admit it. Everybody knew he was inexperienced and they admired him for admitting that he didn't have enough knowledge on a given subject. When he made a mistake, people rallied around and forgave him. After all, he was one of them; they didn't think of him as a 'politician.' His inexperience was more credible than any presumption that he knew all the answers."

The political managers encouraged cordiality, but not chumminess, toward the press. "We treated the media with respect but we didn't encourage a buddy-buddy relationship," Roberts explained. "We held very few press conferences because we didn't like the mob psychology at those things. A newspaper or TV guy is more likely to go wild at a conference to impress the other reporters. Instead of press conferences, we made Reagan available for private interviews. If a reporter complained that we were not turning the candidate loose at press conferences, we asked him if he wanted a personal interview, and I would set one up that very day. Ron startled a lot of skeptical reporters in one-to-one press interviews. He always tried to have an answer, but when he didn't know something, he didn't try to bullshit the reporter."

Spencer-Roberts made effective use of Reagan's best medium: television. By communicating directly on TV, Reagan hurdled the skeptical press. Reagan's appearances on TV were deliberately kept austere, and the candidate spoke without reading a text. He looked good, but not distractingly so on television. Neither an ideologue nor a professional politican, he sounded eminently reasonable and rightly concerned about big government, high taxes and crime. "I like what he says," one Democrat declared, "and if that man is an extremist, I guess I am, too."

Christopher could exercise no magic, on or off television. California's moderately conservative and pragmatic business establishment supported Christopher because Reagan was considered too volatile a product. But Christopher ran a lackluster campaign, wasting time in the cow towns of Northern California when he could have been reaching millions on TV and radio. The early polls showed that Christopher could beat Pat Brown more handily than Reagan, but the same surveys showed that he trailed Reagan among Republicans.

The Democrats expected Reagan to win the primary and hoped to inherit Christopher's moderate following. To help sink Christopher, Pat Brown's assistants provided material for columnist Drew Pearson and revived an old story—twenty-eight years earlier, Christopher, who owned a dairy, had been arrested, fingerprinted and fined for violations of price regulations. Copies of a swarthy, scowling Christopher in a police photograph circulated throughout the state, and the indignant ex-mayor accused Brown and Reagan staffers of engineering a smear. Reagan denied any knowledge of it, but Brown admitted that one of his assistants had helped Pearson. The governor, who said he knew nothing about the police picture, professed shock and personally apologized to Christopher. But the damage was complete—Pat Brown lost all hope of picking up Christopher voters in the general election.

The governor should have paid more attention to his own primary, where Sam Yorty was mounting a potent challenge. Assured by polls that he led the Los Angeles mayor by two to one, the governor concentrated on Ronald Reagan. But Yorty's true strength does not show up in polls. Yorty Democrats resented Brown for his stand on racial problems, and many were blue-collar workers who concealed their feelings from their union leadership. Yorty appealed to the anti-Brown Democrats because he too has been an "againster" all his life. In a thirty-year career, in which he has run for a dozen offices, Yorty has been perpetually embattled on behalf of "the Little Guy" against some vaguely defined conspiracy. He has the kind of tunnel vision that perceives enmity where there is only disagreement, and he is popular in Southern California, where he capitalizes on the deepseated distrust of government.

Like Reagan, Yorty is a creature of television. He has an apple-pie, eternal "ingénue" face with a startling streak of silver in his hair. His flat, adenoidal voice can eviscerate an opponent, and he invariably picks a fight with someone bigger. Even when he is taking his lumps, Sam Yorty looks good on television because he is agile and remembers to smile. In the primary he tore away at Brown and made the Republicans' job easier by recalling the 1964 fair-housing fight. (He and Brown were on the same side of the fair-housing controversy, but Yorty was less vociferous.) When the Watts riot broke out, Yorty quickly blamed Brown and urged tougher police measures. He did not suffer in the polls, although he had left the city twice during the riot to make speeches. Although he junkets around the world, the mayor did not go near Watts during or immediately after the riot. He managed to divert attention from his own mistakes by criticizing the Democratic leadership.

The mayor reminded Democrats that Pat Brown had injected accusations of bigotry into the Proposition 14 fight. Exploiting the notion that government was frustrating the people, Yorty accused the California Supreme Court of delaying, for political reasons, a decision declaring Proposition 14 to be unconstitutional. The court issued its 5-2 decision a few weeks after Yorty's accusation. Following the decision, the white backlash focused on Brown because he had been so prominently identified with the fight against Proposition 14; now that the Supreme Court had ruled against the amendment, as Brown predicted, it reminded the voters that the governor had been impolitic enough to call its proponents bigoted. The court was fixed in the public consciousness as "Pat Brown's court."

All the dissatisfied Democrats rallied around Yorty: oldsters whose savings were eroded by inflation and property taxes; Mexican-Americans who felt Pat Brown was ignoring them for Negroes; workingmen who felt their all-white neighborhoods threatened. The mayor formed an alliance of convenience with another Democrat, Assembly Speaker Jesse Unruh, whose staff provided Yorty with organizational support in Los Angeles County.

Brown's strategists failed to gauge the intensity of feeling against the governor and decided to save their money for the general election. Because of the mayor's

inroads among conservative Democrats, the party registered voters "selectively," concentrating on liberal and
minority neighborhoods and avoiding the Dixiecrat en-
claves in Southern California. But the strategy failed.

On June 2, Yorty got 991,088 votes, nearly 39 per cent of
the Democratic total; Pat Brown got 1,355,262. Meanwhile Ronald Reagan buried Christopher 1,417,623 to
675,683. The governor was badly shaken by Yorty's
strength and the fact that Reagan's total exceeded his
own, although Democrats outnumbered Republicans
three to two. "I've never had an easy fight in my life,"
Pat Brown insisted. "The tougher they are, the better
I like it." The governor blamed the polls for mislead-
ing him, but he lacked conviction.

9

The Democratic Debacle

In 1966, anyone could have beaten Pat Brown. Let's face it, the voters were tired of him. If I had known how far behind I was, I might have gone fishing.
> —Edmund G. Brown, after the Reagan landslide

I wouldn't say I flipped over him, but he did seem awfully nice. Maybe a little square, but a nice square.
> —A West Los Angeles housewife who attended a Reagan rally

Following the primary, Pat Brown realized the extent of California's disenchantment with him—and he panicked. The governor shook up his campaign organization, brought in another manager and called for new polls to see what went wrong. "I tell you," he complained, his fleshy fists pumping in frustration, "when I think of that guy becoming governor, I can't sleep at night."

As the summer wore on, Brown found it harder to sleep, and he lost the old campaigner's zest that he had displayed in 1958 and 1962. More important, he knew he was doing badly on television compared to Reagan. "I don't know what happens when I get in front of those television cameras," he lamented. "It brings out the German in me. I look hard and mean. And those jowls. That damned TV makes 'em look baggier!" Against Knowland and Nixon, Brown had won a sympathy vote as the rumpled, nearsighted Everyman challenging political titans. To counter the appeal of an attractive newcomer, Pat Brown dieted and swam daily in the pool at the governor's mansion until he had lost 20 pounds. He knew that Californians like their chief executive lean and dynamic, but Pat Brown was sixty-one and he looked it. Despite his weight loss, he looked squat and flabby next to Reagan, who seemed considerably younger than the six-year difference in their ages.

Fred Dutton, Brown's one-time cabinet secretary, arrived from Washington to revive the campaign. Dutton is a member of the University of California's Board of Regents and a former Assistant Secretary of State. He shared leadership in the campaign with a hastily assembled Directorate that included Hale Champion, state director of finance, and Don Bradley, Brown's campaign manager of record and the architect of his 1962 victory over Nixon. After the primary no one in Brown's campaign was certain who gave the orders, and the three co-leaders were barely on speaking terms by November. Dutton did most of the talking for Brown.

"We can go a long way toward neutralizing Reagan's

popularity," he reasoned, "if we can show that he is using a dressed-up Goldwater speech. We hope that the
longer Reagan talks, the more he will wear thin on those
who see him as a moderate. People are quietly impressed
by the inexperience argument, but in some ways it
makes it tougher for us. He is a virginal candidate with
no public record to snipe at. And we have to make it
clear that we are talking about inexperience. If we go
too hard on his acting background, it might look as if we
are picking on actors as a profession.

"We have to show what's behind the shining image he
projects, to demonstrate that Reagan is a shallow guy
who had never done any hard thinking about his position. Even George Murphy has a lot of depth, compared
to Reagan. At least Murphy worked for years in the
party before he became a candidate.

"That Good Guy look will wear thin when we show
Reagan is an impulsive guy who blows his top with little
provocation whenever he gets out from under the wing
of Spencer-Roberts. When he pops off, we'll be there
with cameras and microphones. He reacts like a typical
right-winger who sees the world as a conspiratorial
place. He has an entourage of bodyguards that follow
him wherever he goes, while Pat travels like a private
citizen. If we can make these points, we can pull the
Democrats back into the fold."

The Democrats' chief researcher in the "anti" campaign, Harry Lerner, a San Francisco public-relations
man, warned, "We run rough campaigns in California,
and we intend to test Reagan's mettle. It will be rough,
but we can prove everything we say. We have to go hard

on the right-wing thing because he is coming across as a moderate. If we can't stick the right-wing label on him, then we've had it. Without that, it will be a fresh face against a two-term governor."

After eight years Pat Brown had antagonized both liberals and conservatives, and legislators in his own party ridiculed him in public. To be effective, a governor must demonstrate that he is precisely *not* what he is paid to be: a compromiser working with a variety of options. Californians like a resolute chief executive, and Pat Brown, raised in the horse-trading school of politics, was not molded to a larger-than-life dimension. His press conferences revealed him as an imperfectly briefed administrator who stumbled over his own syntax; he groped through ill-comprehended position papers like a man flailing through a thicket. Pat Brown was castigated by legislators and editorialists as a man who loved the trappings of office but hesitated to exercise the leadership inherent in his position. He agonized through decisions—and then changed them. In Sacramento, he was known as "the Tower of Jell-O." Despite the criticism, Pat Brown remained a warm and gregarious human being, deeply proud of twenty-three years of service to his native state. He felt uncomfortable around people who expected a governor to be more than mortal and, in less pressing times, he even kidded about his own lack of charisma. Campaigning in ultraconservative Orange County, he cracked, "The people here have consistently refused to recognize my greatness."

Despite his refusal to take himself seriously, Pat Brown had established a solid and progressive record.

In its early years the Brown administration had a vigor comparable to the early New Deal, and its heady mix of idealism and activism translated itself into public works and services for California.

Pat Brown pushed through a $1.75-billion California Water Project, a far-seeing Master Plan for Higher Education, a Fair Employment Practices Commission and a Consumer Counsel's office. His administration also expanded social welfare programs, originally begun in the Earl Warren era, to help the elderly, needy, infirm, mentally ill and retarded. But in a surprisingly short time the administration acquired the weary look of a party that has been too long in power. Pat Brown kept the state free of major scandal, but there were complaints about political appointments of judges, dispensations of savings and loan charters and the tapping of state employees for political contributions.

When Pat Brown tried to crack down on the intraparty factions he was accused of bossism; when he let the blocs battle it out he was accused of being wishy-washy.

The governor tried to exercise restraint over the volunteer California Democratic Council, but the war in Vietnam infuriated the volunteers. The Council's president, Simon Casady, traveled across California, criticizing President Johnson and the war. Casady, a militant and articulate publisher of a weekly newspaper, said it was a mark of personal courage for a young man to burn his draft card in protest. Soon the phone was ringing from the White House to the governor's mansion, and Casady recalls that Brown asked him to ease up.

"Why don't you talk about the state issues, Si?" The State Department arranged a special briefing in Washington for Casady, but the publisher returned as anti-war as ever.

Brown called for Casady's resignation and the California Democratic Council met in Bakersfield and ousted Casady. The vote split the party's largest volunteer group, and some members resigned after noting that Casady had been penalized for expressing what the Council had been saying in resolutions. It was no secret that Pat Brown and State Controller Alan Cranston had twisted arms unmercifully to engineer the vote against Casady. They dangled state jobs and threats to reduce the once-potent CDC to a group of empty rhetoricians who traded principle for a piece of the action and ended up with neither.

Meanwhile, the governor further aroused the liberals by trying to placate Mayor Yorty. While the mayor checked the polls, he encouraged both sides to compete for his endorsement. Reagan and Brown received separate invitations to lunch with the mayor. Both affairs received widespread television coverage. "I'm going courting for the first time in years," the governor commented, and added lamely, "It's just like courting a beautiful woman." The mayor just smiled. When Reagan came to lunch he reminded Yorty that Brown still hadn't apologized for calling the mayor a paranoid in the primary. The mayor nodded in front of the TV cameras.

Brown went further in his efforts to appease the mayor. When the mayor asked him to seek passage of an

anti-riot bill, the governor agreed, although the legislation was clearly unconstitutional. "It will make Sam
happy and it can't do any harm," the governor said. But
Sam Yorty remained inscrutable. Even if he had endorsed Brown, there was no guarantee that he could
swing to Brown Democrats who voted for him. So to re-
gain the Yorty Democrats, Brown moved toward the
Right. He maneuvered his director of social welfare into
resigning and announced a massive job program to pare
down the welfare rolls. He also proposed an anti-crime
program to answer complaints about rising crime and
court decisions inhibiting police. But Yorty remained
publicly on the fence while he covertly gave Reagan assistance.

In August the Democrats unloaded their bombshell
on Reagan, a twenty-nine-page, slick-paper documentary entitled "Ronald Reagan, Extremist Collaborator."
It declared: "Ronald Reagan is the extremists' candidate
for governor of California.

"He is the extremists' collaborator in California.

"He endorses their projects, promotes their policies,
takes their money.

"He is their 'front man.'

"Meanwhile, he pretends he is a moderate, middle-of-
the-roader.

"The record belies him.

"It shows:

"That he has collaborated directly with a score of top
leaders of the super-secret John Birch Society.

"That his campaign organization is riddled with
members of the Society.

"That he supports the programs, policies and projects of numerous extremist fronts.

"That extremist money from California and Eastern states is an important source of his campaign financing.

"That he uses his acting skill and TV charm to soft-sell the doctrines of radical rightists who condemn Social Security and other social advances as Communist-inspired.

"It is true that genuine conservatives also support Reagan. But they do not call the shots, they bring respectability to a political campaign whose true nature, exposed in this document, will dismay moderates and conservatives of both political parties. . . ."

They supplemented the material with a compilation of quotations from Reagan's past as a speechmaker and ideologue:

Unemployment insurance: "It provides prepaid vacations for a segment of our society which has made it a way of life."

Old-age public assistance: "A faceless mass waiting for handouts."

The Right: "The right wing has a bad image. It's funny, people think of them as obstreperous and objectionable. But I don't see them at lie-ins, or teach-ins at the White House. They call for the impeachment of Earl Warren. I don't agree with them. I don't agree with him, either. I think he's a lousy justice. But at least they're proposing something that's provided for in the Constitution."

The John Birch Society: "I don't believe I have any moral justification for repudiating them."

Federal Aid to Education: "I oppose federal aid to education because no one has been able to prove the need for it."

Income tax: "The entire graduated income tax structure was created by Karl Marx. It has no justification in getting the government needed revenue."

Student demonstrators: "I'd like to harness their youthful energy with a strap."

Vietnam: "We should declare war on North Vietnam. We could pave the whole country and put parking stripes on it, and still be home by Christmas."

Conservation: "A tree is a tree. How many more do you need to look at?"

Developing African nations: "When they have a man for lunch, they *really* have him for lunch."

His qualifications: "Gee, I don't know. I've never played a governor before."

But the bombshell never exploded. Spencer and Roberts knew that the Democrats would use the extremist issue and briefed Ron on what to expect. Reagan ignored the documentary. Months before the Democrats had launched their attack, Spencer and Roberts released a mimeographed statement criticizing the founder of the Birch Society, Robert Welch, but avoiding a blanket indictment of the Society. It was a delicate and effective maneuver that eased the moderates' anxiety about Reagan, but it did not alienate the Birchers and their sympathizers, who were among Reagan's most dedicated supporters. "We could not have Ron repudiate the Society as Nixon did in 1962," said Roberts, "because everyone would have seen through that, and

Ron would have lost credibility. If he had become 'Mr. Expedient,' he would have lost the activists but he would not have gained anywhere else. The Democrats would still have hit him with the Birch issue by planting the idea that he was accepting back-door support from them."

Some of the liberals had to swallow their distaste because the right-wing scare campaign smacked of McCarthyism. Moreover, two weeks before the Democrats released their "extremist dossier," they put on a carnival that weakened their own case. In July, State Controller Alan Cranston, who was Brown's heir presumptive, announced that he possessed a document of undercover anti-Semitic activities in the Birch Society. The controller said his findings (which rehashed material already made public) were so crucial that he felt compelled to deliver it personally to Reagan.

After several days trying to catch Reagan in front of the television cameras, Cranston confronted him at Sacramento Airport. While the TV cameras recorded the scene, Cranston said he wanted to make certain that Reagan understood the true nature of the Society. The candidate took the material and handed it to an assistant, then coldly brushed off Cranston: "All right, you've made your grandstand play. Now why don't you run against your opponent?"

The airport "confrontation" weakened Brown's subsequent attempts to make the extremist issue credible, and Cranston himself seemed a bit embarrassed by the circus. Red-baiting, a political pastime of the Nixon era, had given way to Birch-baiting, but the Democrats were not as adroit at it. They tarnished themselves with a comic opera that could have been rivaled only if Reagan had sent an emissary to thrust a copy of the Communist *People's World* into Pat Brown's hands.

Each of the Democrats' blockbusters fizzled, chiefly because Reagan's handlers anticipated the attack and forewarned the candidate. When the "dossier" came out, Reagan dismissed it: "I've heard of guilt by association, but this must be guilt by disassociation." With an adroit phrase he blunted an attack that had been months in the making, just as George Murphy had done in 1964.

Throughout the campaign Reagan countered questions about the Birch Society by referring to the basic statement about Welch and repeating, "If anybody decides he wants to vote for me, he has bought my philosophy; I haven't bought his." Spencer and Roberts carefully steered Reagan into the unimpeachable middle by arranging a visit to Dwight D. Eisenhower's home in Gettysburg, Pennsylvania, after the primary. The former President told reporters that he was impressed by the candidate's "great integrity and common sense, and I know he's a Republican and I'm for all Republicans." By getting the endorsement of the GOP's most popular figure, Spencer and Roberts removed the reservations of most moderate Republicans.

"We surrounded him with a lot of new young fellows on the way up," said Bill Roberts, "because we wanted to present Ron as a positive guy. We kept him away from the old-fogy element. We didn't encourage the kind of hysteria that attached itself to the Goldwater campaign. In 1964 you saw a lot of feverish people working for

Goldwater. Every Goldwater volunteer was hoarse and red-eyed. We deliberately kept our campaign low-key and friendly. We wanted a nice friendly buzz around the headquarters, but none of that Holy War feeling. We weren't going to give the Democrats anything to hang their extremist charges on.

"I don't think Reagan ever was a real right-winger. Well, maybe he leans to the right, but what's wrong with that? He certainly isn't a fanatic. In fact, he sounded a lot more reasonable than Pat Brown. We didn't have to do too much to change his image because the public didn't think of him as a right-wing radical—only the Democrats did. Anyway, Ron had been saying things that a lot of people felt, so it didn't really hurt when the Democrats brought out their Reagan quotes. We kept the campaign on a positive basis, and the voters accepted Ron as an honest-to-goodness moderate."

Reagan also clarified his differences with Goldwater. He was for unemployment insurance and Social Security, and he opposed right-to-work as "too big a gun for the problems that we want to correct." He avoided questions of national survival and confined himself to state issues.

"The Democrats showed they were out of touch by going so hard on right-wing extremism," said Bill Roberts. "In 1966 the Birchers weren't throwing Molotov cocktails and hitting policemen; the Negroes were. You might disagree with the Birch Society, even disagree violently, but they weren't practicing violence to get their viewpoint across. Besides, we learned in the 1964 Rockefeller campaign that it's tough to put over the right-wing issue. Most people don't know how to define an extremist; the average Bircher looks, acts and talks pretty much like everybody else. If you meet him, say, at a cocktail party, you're not going to start looking for a bomb shelter. The Bircher isn't identifiable, but the Negro is. When California was worried about Negro rioters, Pat Brown was talking about Birchers. When the Democrats got wise and went to inexperience as their main issue, it was too late."

Spencer and Roberts, who handle only Republicans, speculate that they would have run Brown's campaign differently. "Pat should have concentrated on reselling himself instead of tearing down Ron," said Stu Spencer. "There was plenty the governor could point to in eight years. He could have said Ron was a nice guy but he can't be trusted to carry the ball. By going all out to get Ron, they helped him.

"Right after the primary, the governor should have taken some in-depth surveys to see where he really stood. Instead, he reacted too soon. His campaign took off like a skyrocket in July and it stayed that way all summer. Pat was all over the place, and we couldn't keep up with him. We didn't even try."

When the Democrats turned to Reagan's inexperience, which had been their best issue all along, they mishandled that too, by letting it degenerate into an attack on the acting profession. The Democrats offended Hollywood (which is overly sensitive anyway), and they compounded their blunders by the incredibly insensitive tactic of using *actors* to knock the idea of actors' running for public office. One television spot showed an official-looking building, which was later exposed as an impressive façade on a movie set. An even more unsubtle advertisement showed Reagan looking absurd in a Civil War uniform with boots and sword. The attack was so heavy-handed that one actor, Jack Palance, walked out of a Democratic telethon and complained, "Attack him if you wish for his lack of experience, but don't go after him just because he is an actor."

By the end of the campaign Brown had agitated most of Hollywood, which is heavily weighted with liberal Democrats but hesitant about attacking one of its own, especially if he is a winner. (After the election, television star Robert Vaughn, a liberal who opposes the war in Vietnam, sent Reagan a congratulatory telegram: "You have covered yourself with dignity.")

The actor issue is a good one, reasoned campaign manager Don Bradley in a classic misjudgment, "Because it goes over big with the farmers in the San Joaquin Valley, the guys who think an actor isn't a man's man." But elections in California are decided in cities, not farm areas.

In the final weeks the Democrats flooded the air waves with spots from entertainers: "I've played many roles before the camera," actor-dancer Gene Kelly declared. "I've been a soldier, a gambler and even a major-league baseball player. I know I could *play* the role of a governor but I could never really sit in his chair and make decisions affecting the education of millions of children."

The Democrats imported a documentary expert, Charles Guggenheim, from Washington, to produce a

thirty-minute film showing Brown as a crusading district attorney and a compassionate chief executive.
Guggenheim, who worked for Robert Kennedy in New
York, examined thousands of film clips in a few months
and compiled a brilliant documentary—but it was
marred by a scene that lasted less than five seconds: Pat
Brown accosts a group of Negro children and jovially
declares, "I'm running against an actor, and you know
who shot Lincoln, don'tcha?"

The scene raised one of those pseudo-furores that
develop late in a campaign when all the issues are
exhausted. The racial mood of California was so tense,
and Hollywood so resentful, that Brown's crack was
interpreted as an incitement to racial hatred and a slur
on actors. The Republicans rose up in righteous anger
demanding that the offending portion be removed, but
instead the Democrats turned the vignette into a one-
minute TV spot and showed it around the clock in the
last week. "They could have deleted the scene and
ended the hassle," said Bill Roberts, "but they were too
stubborn or locked-in to realize the public reaction. It
made Pat look like a know-nothing. If it were my candidate, I would have made him apologize and leave it at
that."

At any rate, Pat Brown had already lost his credibility
in August at the Democratic Party Convention, when he
told surprised delegates that he would appoint a bipar-
tisan commission to suggest revisions in the Rumford
Act. The delegates booed as their leader, who once
hailed the bill as a major advance, backed away from
what had become a major cause to California liberals.

The about-face did not gain Brown support among conservative Democrats, who remembered his remarks about bigotry in 1964, and it diminished his liberal base.

The convention also revealed Brown's ineptness; he had promised to support Mrs. Carmen Warschaw for party chairman. Mrs. Warschaw, who was then Southern California chairman, had many enemies in the party, including some in Brown's inner circle. Brown gave her a lukewarm endorsement, his campaign manager voted for her opponent and Mrs. Warschaw lost by a vote of 447 to 443.

Mrs. Warschaw, who is known as "the Dragon Lady," did not earn that nickname for nothing. "I knew that Pat Brown would stab me in the back," she cried, "but I wanted to get that sonofabitch on record. How do you like that guy? You mean the governor can't swing four votes, not even the vote of his campaign manager?"

Mrs. Warschaw blew up when she telephoned the governor and learned that Pat, at that moment, was giving a victory celebration for her opponent, Assemblyman Charles Warren of Los Angeles. "I just want to thank you, Governor, for your fucking support," she yelled over the telephone. "Carmen," Brown huffed, "you can't talk to the governor that way." But Mrs. Warschaw was not awed by high office. "With friends like you, I don't need enemies."

A few weeks later Ronald Reagan came calling at Mrs. Warschaw's home and, afterward, without directly endorsing him, she said, "I found Mr. Reagan to be a very moderate kind of person, not at all like what I had been led to believe." What about those condemnatory

Reagan statements issued under her name as Southern California's party chairman? "Oh," said Mrs. Warschaw, "those were releases put out by the organization. Harry Lerner [the anti-Reagan researcher] asked me to sign them, so I did."

While the Democrats fought like alley cats, Reagan maintained his smiling, remote image. When he tackled questions from the crowd he invariably asked, "Now does that answer it for you?" When hecklers laughed at him, he pleaded, "Now hear me out," and won over the audience.

In his personal appearances, he mixed his usual brand of moralizing with playful digs at Pat Brown. He invoked a vision of "The Creative Society" (a phrase suggested by a right-wing radio evangelist) and soared to lyrical heights in what might be called the old Warner Brothers tradition: "A wind is blowing across this state of ours. And it is not only wind; it will grow into a tidal wave. And there will be a government with men as tall as mountains." As he spoke, the audience hushed, their eyes glazed in anticipation, as if the windy rhetoric would part the clouds, revealing Mount Rushmore in the background.

When he decided to go for laughs, he did so cautiously, fearful of confirming the "lightweight" accusation.

"Pat Brown," he said, "uses a microphone as a shoehorn to put his foot in his mouth." Could he think of anything good to say about Pat Brown? "Well, he is good to his family . . . he's put a lot of relatives on the payroll." Reagan warned that Pat Brown, "with mud dripping up to his armpits, will tell us that this is the dirtiest campaign ever!" And: "The governor is talking so much about *his* water that I've been wondering what he's going to do when he leaves: take his water with him? In November we're going to cut his water off!"

He brought the crowd to its feet, stamping and cheering, with a fiery windup: "No, don't vote for me as someone who is going to go up there and line up all the political hacks and cronies and then set out to issue orders and create bureaus and agencies as the answers to the problems.

"Vote for me if you believe as I do that we have here within our borders the greatest people in all this nation and all this earth, and we have attracted them from every state and from every nation. We have the highest level of professional skill and education and training. There isn't anything that we cannot do if we are given a chance to do it. We can be number one not only in population but we can be number one, period. And we can start a reform that will sweep this country like a prairie fire. That's what we can have as a Creative Society in California."

Between appearances Reagan worked on his speech, shuffling his BASICO research cards, and underlining key phrases with a felt-tip pen. This conspicuous display of the author at work served a twofold purpose: it reinforced the image of Reagan acting as his own speech writer, and it prevented intimate contact with reporters.

The California press traveled with the candidate and saw each campaign triumph repeated with mechanical precision down to the last gesture, and it was suspicious

of Reagan from the start. "They are all against me,"
Reagan confided to a friend, "I just know it." And, in a
sense, he was nearly right, but the antipathy worked
both ways; the press considered him a phony and he regarded them as flabby and biased liberals.

He kept reporters at arm's length throughout the
campaign, while Pat Brown enjoyed an old-shoe famili-
arity with the press. When Brown reversed his position
(a frequent occurrence during the campaign), reporters
chided him and he laughed in genial embarrassment.
With Pat it was a game: win a few, lose a few. But Reagan was something else—it was inconceivable for the
press to kid with him or even try to penetrate his rigid
defenses. Everything about Reagan irritated the reporters—his pomposity, quick changes in mood, mechanical smile and, above all else, his air of moral superiority. They bored in with blood in their eyes on the few
occasions when he permitted press conferences.

Spencer and Roberts banned all press conferences
late in the campaign after a potentially disastrous incident in the small lumber town of Chico in Northern California. At a motel, Reagan chatted with reporters and
the discussion turned to the Rumford Act. After a series
of questions Reagan acknowledged that perhaps gov-
ernment-financed housing and multiple units should be
subject to anti-discrimination statutes. Did this not conflict with his declaration that government must not interfere with the individual's right to dispose of property
as he chooses? Reagan squirmed in the sunlight. "I
know I can sit down and straighten this out in my mind."
It was the kind of mixup that Pat Brown would have

laughed off. But Reagan became angrier as he tried to extricate himself. "I'm not sure I know what I'm talking about, I'm so pooped," he said, his face flushed. When the reporters persisted, Reagan turned on them. "You're boring in, aren't you? You're boring in because you know you've caught me so pooped that I don't know what I'm doing." Then he got up abruptly, pleaded exhaustion and left. "You'll be a lot more tired when you're governor," one reporter called after him.

A quick consultation with Spencer and Roberts defused the matter. Reagan explained the next day that "I just goofed. I was too tired to think." The voters made allowances for mistakes that would have been considered intolerable if committed by a "professional politician." Reagan could do no wrong in 1966. When he twice got confused about the location of the Eel River in flood-devastated Northern California, the voters considered his mistake understandable.

This protective attitude toward Reagan disturbed Pat Brown. "What are his excuses?" he asked. "One time he laughs boyishly—no mean trick at our ages—and says he 'goofed.' Another time he admits to being 'too pooped' to think straight, and this was at three-thirty in the afternoon. You can't afford a governor like that. You don't get retakes as governor. Everybody is going to make some mistakes, but you can't make very many in this job. I have never faced an opponent who was so wrong about so many things—not just in matters of opinion but in matters of fact."

The incident at Chico was an exception to Reagan's general policy, anyway; he did not dwell on the Rumford Act, and throughout the campaign he discussed seemingly unrelated subjects. But everyone in California got the point. In a radio spot he declared: "Every day the *jungle* draws a little closer." The jungle? "Our city streets are *jungle* paths after dark, with more crimes of violence than New York, Pennsylvania and Massachusetts combined." Whenever he used "jungle," in the backlash context of 1966, it touched a nerve, especially among low-income whites who lived near the ghettos. Although he treaded somewhat carefully on the racial question, Reagan felt no inhibition about the University of California and, for the first time, the University became part of a political campaign. Since its founding, the University, which is tax-supported, has been open, free of tuition, to all California students in the top one-eighth of their high-school graduating class. It is unquestionably one of the finest and most comprehensive universities in the world and it has repaid the taxpayers many times over in terms of the scientists, professionals and educators it has produced through the years.

Before the primary, during BASICO's trial run with Reagan, Plog and Holden had discovered that the University was a "sleeper issue." "We were getting questions all over the state from people worried about the protests at Berkeley," Plog said. "Wherever we went, people wanted Reagan to say how he would handle the student uprising at Cal." Holden prepared an eleven-page memorandum on Berkeley and its problems, and further study showed that Berkeley was second only to Watts as an issue.

The issue arose from the fact that in the last few years

the University has contended with a growing radical movement at Berkeley, the most prestigious of its nine campuses. Berkeley, which then had approximately 27,000 students in a University-wide enrollment of nearly 90,000, has a considerable social problem because it is the locus for a growing number of adult drifters and hangers-on who aid and incite campus protests. In the Sixties the Berkeley campus became increasingly important as a staging area for civil-rights demonstrations in San Francisco and Oakland. The Bay Area community, one of the most sophisticated in the nation, has tolerated, if not approved of, Berkeley's radical tradition for years. But the University began to be openly criticized in 1964, when anti-Goldwater Republicans recruited students on campus for a demonstration outside the GOP convention in San Francisco's Cow Palace.

The complaints mounted after the students picketed the Oakland *Tribune* to protest alleged discriminatory hiring. The *Tribune* is owned by former Senator William F. Knowland (Goldwater's campaign chairman in California) and, fearing that the demonstration might ignite Oakland's large and militant Negro community, Knowland complained to the Berkeley administration, which decided suddenly to enforce long-disregarded rules about on-campus political activity.

This led to a series of student demonstrations, sit-ins, lock-outs and the now famous Free Speech Movement of 1964, culminating in the dismissal of Berkeley's chancellor and the sudden elevation to fame of a young philosophy student named Mario Savio. "He used to go by the name of Robert Savio in New York," an administration official explained, "but he changed it out here. I guess 'Mario' had a more Garibaldi ring to it."

Berkeley is the only campus in the United States which has full-time reporters from four daily newspapers assigned to it, and the demonstrations attracted television cameramen and reporters as well. The publicity had a self-reinforcing effect on the demonstrators; the more exposure, the more militance. And, invariably, the far-out in sandals and flowing robes, many of them nonstudents, crowded in front of the cameras to frighten middle-class California TV audiences each night. At the heart of the Berkeley protest was a small core of radicals, students and nonstudents, who used campus-wide grievances to stir a much wider following. The complaints of the students were, in many cases, justified, as the administration conceded. Essentially they were the same complaints that could be made about California: the University had become a victim of its own success and was too big, impersonal and remote.

After the Free Speech Movement died down, the investigators moved in. The State Senate Sub-Committee on Un-American Activities issued a lurid 153-page report that lumped Communists, radicals, hippies and sexual perverts on campus and blamed the University president, Dr. Clark Kerr, for not repressing the social deviants.

Ironically, the campus turmoil had faded somewhat by the time Reagan started riding the Berkeley issue (although there was a brief, farcical revival of the disorders in a "Filthy Speech Movement," in which oddballs paraded around with obscene signs). Clark Kerr was making progress, halting but steady, in containing the protests within an orderly framework while maintaining the campus tradition of free speech. Dr. Kerr could make some gains after 1964 because the campus activists had nowhere to go: the civil-rights movement had died and Vietnam protests were merely exercises in frustration. But Reagan's assaults gave the New Left a sense of power. "Preservation of free speech," he declared, "does not justify letting beatniks and advocates of sexual orgies, drug usage and filthy speech disrupt the academic community and interfere with our universities' purpose." He spoke darkly about events at rallies staged by the Anti-Vietnam Day Committee "so contrary to the accepted code of morality that I can't even discuss with you in detail what has gone on." (But while Reagan was publicly taking the high road and viewing with proper alarm, his press secretary, Lyn Nofziger, helped out curious reporters by showing them a sensational and minutely detailed report of an undercover investigator about alleged sexual perversions at an anti-war rally at Berkeley. "Oh, Ron wouldn't dream of using this in the campaign," said Nofziger, "but we're showing you this so you will know what he's talking about." For anyone who couldn't get the drift of Reagan's vague and intriguing references, Nofziger was more than happy to fill in the blank spaces.)

When Reagan's campaign experts got feedback reports about the public's anxiety over the happenings at Berkeley, they knew they had a "gut issue." The University had always been a proud monument in California's tradition, and it had been virtually sacrosanct (although some theoreticians of the Right had opposed the philosophic concept of a free, tax-supported University in competition with private institutions). Now the University was clearly vulnerable, and so, by implication, was the Brown administration. "We can get some of these Rotary Club types to understand that a university has to allow radicals on campus," a Berkeley administrative officer said, "but the talk about pot-smoking and orgies drives them wild."

A number of former Christopher supporters, who went over to Reagan after the primary, asked him to stop his attacks on the University because they feared that partisan criticism would hurt the institution long after the campaign had ended. "My polls show me that the University is a very big issue," Reagan told them, "and I intend to go on talking about it."

To the New Left, which emerged from the Berkeley tumult, Reagan was not the enemy; liberals like Pat Brown and Clark Kerr were. Finally the Far Right and the New Left had a common cause, and each attacked the University from opposite ends. The University had long since learned how to handle attacks from the Right, but the New Left's nuisance value was far more potent.

Like the Right, the New Left complained that Kerr's policies had created a "liberal establishment" which was responsible for the contradictions in education. They saw the University as a link in a conspiratorial directorate of federal government, giant corporations and national foundations. With the paranoia that also afflicts the Right, the New Left treated Cal as a sinister "education factory" that processed students and provided technicians and scientists for an insatiable and impervious War Machine. They wanted to stop the Machine or run it themselves.

"Eventually, we will have a massive confrontation on this campus," a twenty-eight-year-old nonstudent activist, Jerry Rubin, said. "And the campus will have to be closed for months. When it reopens again, if it ever does, Berkeley will never be the same." This was the New Left's plan for Cal—and it hoped to lure the administration into a massive retaliation that would incense the great majority of uncommitted students. Dr. Kerr, who foresaw this strategy, tried to blunt it by avoiding even the appearance of repression, but his undramatic mediator's approach angered the Board of Regents, which had to deal with complaints from the public and the Legislature.

By galvanizing public hysteria and giving Reagan a talking point, the New Left did more than the Right to defeat Pat Brown. And the New Left, which has no historical perspective and no memory of the liberal gains of the Thirties, wanted Reagan to win, reasoning that a conservative would make clear those contradictions that were papered over by liberals like Brown.

The New Left weakened the left wing of the Democratic party by forming a New Politics movement, which drained off anti-war activists from the California Democratic Council. The separatist movement at first was hailed by Pat Brown's advisers, who believed that it would clean the party's skirts of left-wingers and make Brown less vulnerable. But the Democrats forgot about Sam Yorty, who brought up in the primary all the left-wing charges left over from previous Republican campaigns.

When riots erupted briefly in San Francisco and Oakland, they were the last nails in the incumbent's coffin. At first Reagan, succumbing once more to his reckless streak, accused Brown of failure to learn from the Watts uprising of 1965. But Spencer and Roberts, sensing correctly that riots were too tricky an issue, urged a more prudent course because they did not want to confirm Brown's charge that Reagan was exploiting the riots. After that outburst Reagan made only restrained comments on the violence.

"When Pat Brown interrupted his campaign and flew to San Francisco," Roberts said, "we held our breath. We figured he might come up with a dramatic invitation for Ron to join him at the scene of the trouble and take the race issue out of the campaign. If that had happened, I'm not sure what we could have done. If we turned Pat down, it would look like we were rejecting a chance to show unity on an issue that goes beyond politics. If we went along, what the hell could Ron do there anyway? Pat's an old-time district attorney and he could have used the situation to demonstrate his experience and make Ron look bad by comparison. But his people didn't think of that, so we breathed easier after Pat resumed his campaign."

Spencer and Roberts probed every crack and fissure in the old Democratic coalition. The AFL-CIO spent an estimated $3 million to reelect Brown but the investment was wiped out by the rank-and-file's resentment over fair housing. Spencer and Roberts flooded the low-

income white areas in traditional Democratic neighborhoods with a pamphlet recalling Reagan's six terms as
president of the Screen Actors Guild, an AFL-CIO affili-
ate. The pamphlet's title was "Can a Union Man Be
Elected Governor?" It reminded the voters that Reagan
opposed the 1958 right-to-work drive but it did not mention that Reagan also supports Section 14B of the Taft-
Hartley Act which permits states to establish right-to-
work laws. The pamphlet recalled that Pat Brown
sunned himself at Frank Sinatra's home in Palm Springs
when striking Mexican-American grape pickers
marched 300 miles to Sacramento. But it deleted Reagan's description of the march as "an Easter egg roll put
on by professional bleeding hearts."

Spencer and Roberts also capitalized on a huge protest vote siphoned off by Yorty in Mexican-American
areas. The mayor exploited the Mexican-Americans'
feeling that Pat Brown was ignoring them in favor of
Negroes.

The Reagan statewide campaign slogan was "Ya
basta" (Spanish for "Had enough"), and it summed up
the attitude of the proud, insular and anguished Mexican-Americans, who number more than 2 million in California, nearly double the Negro population. Although
the Mexican-Americans traditionally register 90 per cent
Democratic, they have been deprived of a meaningful
voice in California politics. Not a single Mexican-
American sat in the California Legislature in 1966, although there were Negroes in both houses. Los Angeles
has the largest concentration of Mexican-Americans in
the nation, but there are none on the City Council,
though there are three Negroes.

The governor compounded his deteriorating relations with California's largest minority by alienating the most influential Mexican-American in the state, Dr. Francisco Bravo, a wealthy East Los Angeles surgeon and banker. Bravo helped Brown roll up a big margin over Nixon in 1962 but afterward, he recalled, "No one from around here [Bravo presumably meant himself] got invited to the governor's mansion. And not a word about appointments except to crumb jobs. Pat Brown made eighty-four appointments to the Superior Court bench and not one Mexican-American was on the list. I wrote the governor a letter telling him that we weren't getting enough jobs for our people and he replied that he wasn't running an employment agency. He had the nerve to tell me that he made appointments only on the basis of merit. What an insult! Did he feel our people were not qualified to fill important jobs? I sent him a list of qualified individuals, people whose educational accomplishments exceeded his own."

Bravo backed an old friend, Mayor Yorty, and after the primary Pat Brown announced a rash of Mexican-American appointments, which incensed Bravo. "Did we suddenly become qualified? Brown should have done that four years earlier. Now it was doubly insulting because he thought he could buy us at the last minute."

After the primary Mayor Yorty advised Reagan to see Bravo, and the two men talked for four hours in the surgeon's office at his new Pan-American National Bank in East Los Angeles. When Pat Brown heard about the meeting he tried to telephone Dr. Bravo, but it was too late. Bravo, who originated the slogan "Ya basta," ran Reagan's Mexican-American campaign. When he toured East Los Angeles, Reagan was greeted with *abrazos* and cheers.

"Our people like a guy with style," explained William Orozco, who is Reagan's field representative in Los Angeles. "A Mexican-American might wear a dirty shirt but he doesn't want to vote for a guy with one. When Reagan came to East Los Angeles, they saw this big, good-looking guy, a beautiful dresser, with that flashing smile and that great handshake. How could Pat Brown compete with that? Pat kept calling them 'You people,' and saying how much the Democrats were doing for them. He bored hell out of everybody."

When Pat Brown campaigned in East Los Angeles he drove in a motorcade past Dr. Bravo's bank—and held his nose in disdain. "It only made our people work harder," said Dr. Bravo. Reagan cut deeply into the Democratic strength and picked up an estimated 24 per cent of the Mexican-American vote. Pat Brown looked increasingly like a loser. His crowds were small and listless. When he walked through factories the governor saw Reagan stickers on lathes and drill presses. At lunch breaks silent clusters of workmen, wearing large Reagan buttons, stood with arms folded. The governor strained for a light touch: "The polls say I am doing all right with the men but I am way, way down with the women. Now maybe I am missing something, and you gals can help me. They say the women like Ronnie Ree-gin's charm. Now if you girls can give me a few tips, it would really help."

As the campaign closed, he carried on like a good soldier in a losing battle. His campaign bus, an old two-decker, was nearly empty. The governor had ample time to smoke a cigar and reflect. He smiled thinly at the hecklers who taunted him: "What about the left-wing CDC?" "When are you going to do something about taxes?" "What about relatives on the payroll?"

At a luncheon in San Pedro, Pat Brown found four empty seats at his table, and he turned to newspapermen covering his final agonies. "Why don't you fellows join me up here? It's getting lonely." But no one moved. After lunch, as he campaigned on the sidewalk, a long-shoreman asked him to sign a bill for a new freeway link. "I sure hope you can put that freeway across before Reagan gets elected," he told the governor. Pat Brown's face sagged. "Well, I'm not so sure that guy is gonna make it," but he didn't believe it either.

"While I was working for this state, as district attorney, attorney general and, for the last eight years as governor, what was my opponent doing?" he asked audiences. "Well, he was making movies like *Girls' Night Out* and *Bedtime for Bonzo.* Can you imagine turning over this great state to that actor?

"Can anyone tell me one solitary thing that Ronnie Ree-gin has ever done for California? Has he ever spent a day in any of our institutions or hospitals?

"You mothers and fathers out there, how would you feel about paying $1,000 tuition for your son to attend the University? Well, that's what my opponent wants to do."

Pat Brown talked about water, schools and roads, but the voters wanted to know what he would do about riots, welfare, property taxes and the University of California. When the governor tried to answer, no one paid attention. "If he hasn't kept his promises for eight years," asked Reagan, "why should we expect him to do anything in the next four?"

In the final week the governor pleaded: "My friends, we have had eight years of good, sensible, honest government without a breath of scandal. Clean government. Fiscally sound. What has Reagan ever done? Have any of you ever heard him say anything about helping anyone in this state? The retarded child? The conservation camps? The aged? Has anyone ever heard him say how he would make it better for them? My administration has been an administration with a heart: we built schools and took care of the aged and needy.

"Take a look at the record. By any objective measure you will renew my contract for another four years. The people are not going to vote against themselves. You have never seen my opponent fight for California. You have never heard or seen him visiting a park, a Headstart class, a water project, a correctional facility or a mental institution.

"California is a great state, and we cannot afford to turn it over to a man without one day of experience in government. My opponent just doesn't know what he is talking about."

In his political death throes Pat Brown seized on an issue that wiped out Nixon in 1962: Reagan's White House dreams. He had taunted Nixon for weeks by characterizing the former Vice-President as an opportunist "who was double-parking outside the State House to pick up a little political change en route to the White House."

He told his 1966 crowds: "Don't delude yourselves that my opponent's ambitions end in Sacramento. My opponent refuses to deny that he is being considered as a Presidential candidate. He harbors Presidential ambitions." But Spencer and Roberts had anticipated that ploy too, and they sent Reagan's press secretary on two trips to Washington. "If you want to sink Ron," Lyn Nofziger warned conservative columnists in Washington, "the best way in the world is to keep mentioning him as a possible Presidential candidate. The Democrats will say he's planning to run out on his contract with the people of California. They'll blow him right out of the water." The columns speculating about Reagan's Presidential hopes disappeared for the rest of the campaign.

The Democrats had fired everything in their arsenal, and all they had proved was that Pat Brown deserved to lose. The final vote was Reagan, 3,742,913; Brown, 2,749,-174. Reagan won in 55 of California's 58 counties and the voters turned down all but one of the Democratic office-holders. And so the Democrats had slid all the way back to pre-1958 when they could elect only one Democrat, Attorney General Pat Brown, to office.

On the night that Pat Brown lost the governorship he stepped gracefully out of public life, determined not to repeat Richard Nixon's horrendous "farewell press conference." The governor reached into himself to salvage a shred of cheer and thanked California "for giving me eight wonderful, marvelous years." Then, weary and hoarse, he disregarded his advisers, who wanted him to leave by a rear exit—and plunged into the diminished and sad-faced crowd of loyal Democrats to shake hands and rub elbows for the last time. As the Reagans waved to the crowds and the television cameras, the governor sagged in his limousine, shaking with muffled sobs, as an assistant drove him back to his rented mansion in Los Angeles' Hancock Park.

10

The Acting Governor

He's hot right now, but we will have to see how he does as governor. There are a lot more problems when you move up from the Late Show *to the* Early Morning Show.

> —Governor Nelson A. Rockefeller,
> November 8, 1966

In state government, unlike Ronald Reagan's earlier profession, there are no happy endings. The problems are endless, the contradictions tiresome and the details tedious, especially to a man who sees the world in black-and-white terms. The varying shades of gray encountered in the business of government can be a murky and soul-draining experience.

In some ways Reagan's greatest advantage was his complete and blissful ignorance of the governor's problems: and at first he thought of his new job in terms of a personal vindication. Now he could *do* good as well as look and sound good; now he had the kind of role that had always eluded him in the movies, and California would have to take him seriously. But the habits of a lifetime cling tenaciously, and Reagan still thinks and reacts like a man more comfortable with illusion.

At first he had assumed that his landslide was a mandate for sweeping changes, that he could take charge convincingly and sweep California clean of bureaucratic residue and take a giant step toward the ultimate role: the Presidency.

As always, he had to mask his ambitions. On the night he was elected he announced that he would head a favorite-son delegation to the national convention "only to insure party unity." And he dismissed talk of his Presidential hopes with a beautifully timed throwaway line: "I'm not really ambitious *that* way." Every move he has made since that night has confirmed what the insiders long suspected: Sacramento was to be a way station to Washington. But first he had to give a convincing performance as governor.

The outlines of his "Creative Society" program remained fuzzy, as ambiguous as the man himself, all surfaces, angles and shifting lights with nothing at the core. Its direction and content were a triumph of imagery; Reagan made loud noises for a year and brought forth very little that was new, creative or reassuring. He continued to be a master at public relations but he demonstrated that he was a fumbler at the levers of government. For all his shortcomings in style and leadership, Pat Brown had been a builder who would get good marks from historians long after his deficiencies were forgotten. But Reagan, who talked about "lighting

prairie fires," revealed little more than a cramped and
sterile view of public office. However, his gift for glittering rhetoric distracted California while his administration skittered on the edge of disaster in the first months.
To some who predicted a total debacle, the fact that
Reagan had *not* fallen flat on his face made it look as if
he had achieved a triumph of style if not substance. In
any event, the voters did not expect miracles from the
new governor and they liked what they assumed was his
direction, even though he staggered and floundered.

"It was a short honeymoon," the new governor
cracked. "I must have lost my marriage license on the
way to the church." In fact, the honeymoon never
started because both sides continued peppering each
other in the period between election and inauguration, a
time usually devoted to soothing tempers and hurt feelings. Reagan moved up his swearing-in ceremony to
midnight, January 2, and excluded the outgoing governor from the ceremony. Pat Brown had infuriated him
by making eighty judicial appointments in his final days
in office, and Reagan lamented, "I'm probably the only
governor who can't fix a parking ticket."

At the swearing-in, Reagan looked over the solemn
group of officeholders gathered under the Rotunda of
the State Capitol, and spotted U.S. Senator George
Murphy. "Well, George," he cracked on television,
"here we are on the *Late Show* again." Then, in an
abrupt change of mood, he delivered an impassioned
four-minute speech recalling Benjamin Franklin's ob-
servation that politicians should live by the precepts of
the Prince of Peace. "I don't think anyone could ever

take office and be so presumptuous to believe he could do that or that he could follow those precepts completely," the new governor declared in a constricted, emotion-choked voice. "I can tell you this, I'll try very hard. I think it is needed in today's world."

On Thursday of that week the Reagan family rode through sunny but chilly Sacramento to the Capitol Mall, while armed police patrolled rooftops and peered through binoculars at an Inauguration Day crowd of 15,000. Since John F. Kennedy's assassination and the bitter campaigns thereafter, California had been charged with foreboding, and Reagan had been shaken by a number of death threats he received in the mail. (After his inauguration the state increased its security forces in the Capitol and installed a bulletproof window in Reagan's office.)

In keeping with the mood, the governor delivered an austere speech in which he established his chief priority: "We are going to squeeze and cut and trim until we reduce the cost of government." He pledged economies that reflected the mood of his basic constituency, that vast middle-class who comprised Reagan's "forgotten Americans." To the millions of Californians who felt threatened he promised riot-control legislation, a strengthened police force and a crusade against pornography. (Reagan had endorsed an anti-pornography amendment, Proposition 16, during the campaign, and it had failed by 600,000 votes.) To the others most in need of government's help—the poor, the minorities, the old, the infirm, the retarded and the disabled—he promised very little. He and the forgotten majority shared a feel-

ing of solidarity on that chilly day: We versus They; taxpayers against tax spenders. His speech sounded like a
New Deal in reverse. Government would not attack the
causes of social unrest; it would simply repress the
symptoms.

"The time has come," he declared, "to run a check to
see if all the services government provides were in answer to demands or were just goodies dreamed up for
our supposed betterment. The time has come to match
outgo to income, instead of always doing it the other
way around."

Having succeeded as a campaigner, the new chief
executive at first saw no need to change his approach.
He irritated the old hands in the Legislature by lapsing
into the jargon of the campaign to impress the visiting
press:

"Nobody in California has quite realized what we are.
There's nobody quite like us with a thousand different
viewpoints.

"If we can prove that we can take care of our problems here in California, if we can do this thing, we can
say to a lot of people back in the tired East, 'It works,
this system of ours.' If we can give back the people their
courage and their belief in this kind of government by
the people, there is no state in the Union which also
cannot bring off such a thing. . . ."

But after the rhetoric had dissipated it soon became
clear that Reagan was not prepared for the tedium of the
job; he turned over the daily business of governing to his
staff, which struggled with the details that had always
bored him. His inexperienced assistants had to weigh

the problems that transcend class and party: water allocation, pollution, highway priorities and flood control. Reagan, who has not impressed Sacramento with his desire to master the details that are the essence of statecraft, happily let his assistants handle the homework.

As a result, legislators have complained that his palace guard isolated him from the pulse of government. Whenever he met with a legislator or a pressure group, the governor had to be surrounded by assistants. Meanwhile there has been a series of power struggles within the governor's inner circle, and the rivalry intensified as Reagan's Presidential hopes brightened.

Since his inauguration Reagan has let a half-dozen high-ranking assistants resign, including his two most important appointees, Executive Secretary Phil Battaglia, a thirty-two-year-old lawyer who was his 1966 campaign chairman, and Director of Finance Gordon Smith, a Los Angeles management consultant who had no prior experience in government.

The governor's staff at first was divided into "hawks" and "doves," referring to those who wanted Reagan to go on tour and thus stake his claim to the 1968 Presidential nomination, and the minority who thought Reagan's best chance was to concentrate on the governorship. After the first few months the "hawks" clearly had the upper hand in the inner councils; following the departure of Phil Battaglia, Lyn Nofziger, Reagan's "director of communication" (a new and appropriate title in state government), became the number one assistant. Most of those who left the administration have been considered "doves." Nofziger is an avowed "hawk." While Reagan makes out-of-state trips to enhance his Presidential prospects, his staff runs the machinery of government. His new executive secretary, William P. Clark, who was promoted from cabinet secretary, gave reporters an insight into the decision-making process of the Reagan administration: the problems are reduced to one-page memoranda, neatly listing problems, discussion and solution; the governor is required to make only an initialed "ok, rr." Thus the governor can make a dozen or more decisions in a half hour.

As a result there were mutterings about "the *acting* governor," and some Republican legislators grumbled, "He is a presence, not a governor." For the first three months mimeographed statements and sloganeering comprised the vital work of the new team. Each day, the administration issued new statements of shock about the mismanagement of the previous Ins. "We didn't know how bad it was until we got here," Phil Battaglia commented, "and we learned it really was as bad as we said it was."

For a while Reagan could blame everything on the departed Democrats, and he could cite Democrats in the Legislature (the Democrats clung to a 42-38 edge in the Assembly, but were 20-20 in the Senate) for his inability to solve current problems. By continuing the rhetoric of the campaign, the new administration bought time and pacified the electorate, but its partisan announcements irritated and infuriated the Legislature.

The new administration diverted itself by flogging a dead horse: Brown had left the state $194 million in debt, having resorted to questionable accrual accounting by which the state considered as twelve-month income the revenue collected over fifteen months. (The Brown administration, which had to wipe out a cash deficit in its first year, justified this fiscal gimmickry on the grounds that Republicans would not approve meaningful tax reform.)

Reagan went on television and charged that the state treasury had been "looted and drained." The phrase infuriated Republicans as well as Democrats who had voted for the budget. For years Sacramento had had a cozy system in which Republicans and Democrats got together after the election, forgot the oratory and went about the state's business. Now the new governor with the big following was threatening all this. "I'm very distressed," said Assembly Speaker Jesse Marvin Unruh (who can get more mileage out of being distressed than any other politician). "The governor certainly couldn't have meant the dictionary application of the word 'looting.' That implies criminality. I certainly hope that isn't what he meant." At his weekly press conference the new governor conceded he had made a bad choice of words.

Jesse Unruh was the one Democrat who emerged, a bit shaken but still intact, from the Republican landslide of 1966, which he had predicted two years earlier. "It could very well be someone like Reagan in 1966," the Speaker reflected. "He has a lot of support, and if the Republicans are hungry enough to stick together, he could make it." When his old intraparty nemesis, Pat Brown, ran for a third term, Unruh suddenly discovered an unquenchable interest in the Dominican Republic,

Panama and Mexico, and when that thirst was slaked he retired to the unhurried pleasantries of academic life at the Eagleton Institute in New Jersey, where he meditated about the nature of man while Pat Brown joined the legion of losers.

Shortly before the end, Unruh roused himself from his reflections and returned to California, where he made a few perfunctory speeches for Governor Brown. "I think I did all I could for the governor," he said in wide-eyed innocence. "People on my staff helped in his campaign; I made speeches for him. Why, I don't know what else I could have done, except ring doorbells."

The demise of Pat Brown left Jesse Unruh the most powerful Democrat in California, but that may be a questionable honor, because, with a Republican tide running in California, Jesse may have very little to preside over in the next few years. In fact, he almost got caught in the Brown disaster when his obscure Republican opponent ran a surprisingly strong race in the southwest Los Angeles assembly district which is Unruh's base. "Jesse isn't really worried," one Democrat cracked, "but he just might take the ballots home and count them himself, to make sure that nobody tampers with them."

Even Unruh was surprised by the size of Reagan's victory, and he concedes that no politician, including himself, could have beaten Ronald Reagan in 1966.

When Reagan took office the Sacramento hands rubbed their palms in anticipation of what the old pro would do to the new governor. But it didn't work that way, because Unruh, who is gifted with the kind of prescience that makes polls unnecessary, reasoned that Reagan clearly expressed the current mood in California. If he tangled right off with a new and popular governor, he would be stigmatized forever as "the heavy." So Unruh resisted the temptation to get into an open row with the new administration.

At first the other legislators wondered what in hell got into Jesse. When he could say something nice about the new regime, he did; when Reagan bogged down in budget wrangles, he viewed the mess charitably and, with a straight face, voiced the hope that the new team would get over its jitters. And when the governor got enmeshed in meaningless fights with the state bureaucracy, Unruh followed his progress more in sorrow than in anger, looking peacefully resigned amid reflective puffs of cigar smoke.

But that was early in the game, and now Unruh and Reagan are declared enemies. It is an uneven match, because Unruh can outgun the governor in talent as well as experience. He is an old hand at diminishing chief executives, as Pat Brown can attest. In a state cluttered with hyperbole and images, Unruh is a supreme realist who knows where the votes are and how to get them. He admits that he had some skill at raising money and sometimes puts contributors onto the paths of favored politicians. He is California's foremost power broker, and one of the shrewdest legislators in the United States.

The Legislature has always been sensitive about its rights in relationship to the governor's executive branch, and Unruh has exploited that feeling to cement his own position. And when he himself has been unable to move legislators, he has had considerable, but unwitting, help from the Reagan administration, whose impetuosity has irritated nearly everybody in Sacramento.

Reagan has leaped into battles without consulting legislators in his own party; his first finance chief, Gordon Smith, lectured Capitol veterans as though he were giving a class in economics for dull freshmen, and the administration has embarrassed itself with amateurish lies and contradictory statistics. For instance, when the administration tried to cut back the state's Medi-Cal program, pleading a deficit of $210 million as an excuse to eliminate services to the poor, Unruh pounced on Reagan. The administration later admitted that the program actually had a surplus of $30 million, but the concession was grudging all the way, and the governor's team tried to save face with a profusion of figures. The reversals were so blatant that Reagan asked for the resignation of his finance director to appease angry legislators.

Reagan tried to put a smiling face on the mess. "We achieved a surplus because we worked out a number of economies, and the opposition knows it." But Reagan had exposed his amateur standing and Unruh needled him for weeks: "It is clear now that this administration governs by panic without waiting for all the facts before it takes action. No real fiscal crisis in Medi-Cal existed. As I have said before, no business could possibly stay solvent by operating in this unbusinesslike manner. What the governor was really demanding of that session was the ratification of his philosophical opposition to the Medi-Cal program as a whole."

When the Republicans tried to challenge Unruh's leadership in the Assembly, he beat them down on a straight party vote. He relieved two Republicans of their committee chairmanships. "I have no retribution in my soul," he explained nonetheless. "I'm always willing to forgive, if not forget." In the past, before Reagan, Unruh could count on a few Republican votes. "I like to have votes from both sides of the aisle," he commented. "It makes me feel a little more secure. I have seventy-nine colleagues in the Assembly, and the minute forty-one get mad at me I'm through." Unruh was quite used to feuding with the executive branch; he and Pat Brown had had increasingly greater differences over the years.

When Brown had proposed a program, Unruh had come up with an alternative; he always denied that he was trying to embarrass the governor, claiming that he simply wanted the Legislature to develop programs independently. "Yeah, Jesse is real big for good government," Pat Brown's assistants snorted. When Unruh proposed programs that were more progressive than the governor's, Pat Brown attributed it to Unruh's raging ambition. The two men acquired labels that were totally irrelevant to their positions: Unruh became the champion of "conservative" and "moderate" Democrats, Brown the leader of the "liberal" wing. But the Democrats do not have the ideological splits of California's GOP; their feuds are based almost entirely on personality. As Unruh describes it, California's Democratic party has always been a mélange of "feudal duchies and baronies, each with its own leader." What chafed at both men was not their philosophy, but the inability of each to manipulate the other. Their wrangling degenerated into unseemly nit-picking as each office fired mimeographed volleys daily and then fell back; occasionally each would use a third party to make its point, the way the Soviet Union formerly referred to Albania when it meant Red China. "I think that the executive must run the government under the safeguards that the Legislature enacts," Pat Brown declared. "The Legislature has no power except to act as a legislative body. The executive must run the state of California without having to consult committees of the Legislature."

Unruh, who elevated the professional standing of the California Legislature, pleaded against the imbalance of power in the executive. "By and large," he says, "state legislatures, as compared to the executive branch, are weak, lack independence, have a low regard for themselves and are poorly regarded by the citizenry. A governmental body finding itself in this depressed condition is no match for its formal partners in government, the governorship or the courts. Neither is it a match for its informal partners in the governmental process, the press and the organized special interests.

"This presents a dangerous condition for American democracy. It is obvious that a weak legislature cannot exercise an effective check on a strong executive nor can it serve effectively to reconcile the conflicting demands of powerful interests to the satisfaction of the whole society. And so our system, so brilliantly conceived by our founding fathers, breaks down."

The current power and prestige of the State Assembly is Jesse Unruh's crowning achievement, and his accom-

plishments there will remain long after his feuds are forgotten. Unruh's Assembly, a progressive and efficient
body, exemplifies the yeasty ferment of what Unruh
calls "the New Politics," which means that technicians
rather than dogmatists attack long-standing problems—
education, taxation, water allocation, air pollution and
economic diversification. Unruh believes the traditional
liberal-conservative dialogue is neither applicable nor
desirable in finding solutions, and that California must
rely more on professional consultants to handle problems.

In the Legislature, dislike of Reagan runs deep for
reasons of personality as well as tradition; Republicans
and Democrats for years have gotten drunk and raised
hell together, and they resent a glib chief executive who
is hard put to conceal his contempt. When they talk to
Reagan, even at social gatherings, the legislators (who
are not as insensitive as Reagan thinks) get the feeling
that they are being patronized, as if they were fans waiting in line on one of his GE tours. The legislators sat on
their hands on January 9, 1968, when Reagan delivered
his second "State of the State" message. There was no
applause during his thirty-five-minute oration, and
Unruh looked pleased and omniscient as ever.

Unruh's first major break with the new governor occurred midway through the first session, over the issue
of state income tax withholding. Until then the Speaker
had tried to keep a variety of options open so the administration could retreat from untenable positions without
embarrassment (and, more important to Unruh, allow
him to avoid an open conflict with a popular governor).

But Reagan kept boxing himself into tight corners from which it became harder for anyone to extricate him.

Reagan presented a billion-dollar program for increased income, sales, corporate and luxury taxes, but he refused to support a withholding system (although thirty-one out of thirty-four states with a general income tax use it). Although the number two and three Republicans in the state—Lieutenant Governor Robert Finch and Controller Houston Flournoy, both moderates—favored it, Reagan remained opposed on the grounds that "taxes should hurt." California has a revenue gap each year, and Unruh advocated withholding because it would smooth out the flow of income as the state took a percentage from each paycheck instead of a large sum once a year.

In order to relieve the cash flow, the state had to pay ten million a year interest to borrow funds, and California was losing millions each year because its current collection system did not bring in enough money to make it worthwhile to catch evaders. Proponents of withholding argued that California would get an additional $60 to $80 million the year it went into effect.

In light of these facts, would the governor change his mind? "Only if they bound me hand and foot, and held my feet to the fire," Reagan replied. Eventually, besieged by members of his own party, Reagan acquiesced to a compromise as unsatisfactory as the original problem: he agreed to semiannual withholding (which doesn't solve the problem because it simply increases paperwork without smoothing out the cash flow). It was typical of the administration that its grudging retreat on withholding solved nothing but simply postponed the inevitable.

But if all was not going well with the Legislature, at least there was no lack of interest in Ronald Reagan's progress. The new governor attracted packed press conferences, and the Eastern press came West to see California's political phenomenon. Reagan achieves his finest hour each week at the Tuesday-morning press conference, which he handles with crisp professionalism. The governor can hold his own with the Sacramento press corps, and he does not get many questions that his staff has not already anticipated. The question-and-answer procedure is precise and correct, if not cordial, and the reporters are asked to confine their questions to one topic at a time, moving on to the next subject after the previous one is exhausted. When Pat Brown held his press conferences he rambled informally, shuffling papers and generally acting like a man on a hot seat. But Reagan runs the gamut like a man who has been over the jumps and likes the exercise.

He also began a series of televised "Reports to the People"—two-minute taped discourses on current state issues—that were dispatched to California's forty television stations. Two of the films made the CBS Evening News, which meant an audience of approximately 19 million. No governor in California's history had ever mastered the public-relations aspect of the job as well as Reagan.

Meanwhile, the governor's conservative supporters dreamed of the millennium: armed with computers and efficiency charts, Reagan would bring back the Old

Deal, when state government was an appendage of the business community. He would use the arguments of economy to diminish the public sector and re-energize private enterprise. But reality thwarted them because California has thrived under a consortium of corporations and government at both state and federal levels. The state provided technicians and scientists from public universities and colleges to run the aviation and aerospace complex. California's $4.5-billion "agri-businesses," which are "corporatized" farms, profited immeasurably from Democratic water programs and the state's agricultural research. The social welfare sop for the poor and the minorities was a small price for giant corporations to pay for economic stability. In a sense, the Democratic party was the party of big business in California; Reagan's constituency was weighted with marginal entrepreneurs, on whom the cost of government weighed most heavily.

Reagan's mandate came directly from California's anxious new class, which, having struggled up for its place in the sun, failed to see why it should help others achieve the same position. "The forgotten American," said Reagan, "is that fellow living in the suburbs or in a high-rise in the middle of town and is working sixty hours a week to provide the advantages for his family, but is being taxed heavily to take care of some other people's problems."

The governor was speaking for Californians whose own security had been underwritten by collective bargaining, Social Security, workmen's disability, unemployment compensation and Medicare, but in the Sixties it was tougher to convince the comfortable and secure 90 per cent to part with some of its wealth on behalf of the one-tenth that remained ill-fed, ill-clothed and ill-housed.

Reaganism in California was the triumph of the state's 3,700,000 private homeowners, the small businessman and the well-fed blue-collar worker who had been a "pork-chop liberal" in the Thirties. To reassure them Reagan promised to cut the social programs for which they no longer were willing to pay. But because of California's interdependent economy, under which giant businesses support a measure of social welfare, the governor could only make token gestures.

The new administration moved to nail down its original support by trumpeting a series of economies, but, despite the headlines, the savings amounted to less than half of 1 per cent. In his first days in office the governor ordered a temporary hiring freeze on state employees, and directed all state agencies to cut their budgets by 10 per cent. He even sold Pat Brown's beloved propeller transport, the Grizzly II. He reduced out-of-state travel by employees, suspended purchase of new state vehicles and canceled a new $4-million state office building. His assistants estimated the governor had saved $50,000 a year in typewriter ribbons and two million in the state's phone bill. To showcase his image as a determined budgeteer, Reagan told audiences that he had even ordered secretaries in the Capitol to retain the old stationery, cross out Pat Brown's name and type in his own.

He exploited the feeling that the government services were staffed by time-wasters who could not succeed elsewhere, and he talked about throwing out the "political hacks and cronies." But Sacramento's old hands smiled and cleared their desks for bureaucratic warfare; they had been through this kind of siege before. Governors come and go but state employees and lobbyists last forever, and when Governor Reagan asked the state's 163,000 employees to work on Lincoln's and Washington's Birthdays less than 2 per cent showed up. "I just wanted to walk around and see all those smiling, busy faces," the governor explained. He had made his point with the public, but he earned the unremitting enmity of the state work force. More experienced politicians knew better than to tangle with the bureaucracy. When Goodwin J. Knight took office he told his appointees, "Find your desk, get under it and don't raise your head for the next four years—and don't you ever dare get in a hassle with the civil service." State employees, who are highly organized and defensive when attacked, are well aware (even if Reagan was not) that the governor has hardly any political leverage with them.

The idea for state employees to work on the holidays was proposed at one of Reagan's staff meetings. That it was not quashed immediately betrays one of Reagan's weaknesses as an administrator: his inability to weigh or solicit dissenting opinions. An effective administrator normally wants argument, not unanimity, among his assistants—and when everyone agrees, he worries. Sometimes he will even appoint an adviser to play devil's advocate and marshall opposing arguments. But Reagan's staff, like the governor himself, felt most secure when there were no counter arguments.

"Reagan is drawn to decisive types who are very positive in their recommendations," a former consultant said. "He accepts uncritically the theories of men of action, who manage to speak in unqualified terms about getting things done. When Reagan handles a problem with clear-cut alternatives of good and bad, he can be effective, as in the campaign. But government contains so many options that it frustrates anyone who tries to think in absolutes. Reagan doesn't have the knack for weighing alternatives. Once someone has been certified to him as a Good Guy, he finds it hard to believe that this man might do something against the governor's interests, even unconsciously. He favors people who tell him what he wants to hear, but what he needs more than anything else are people who will tell him no.

"The people in his inner circle lack insight and they fail to appreciate other points of view. In many ways they typify their boss's strengths and weaknesses. They form a protective ring that filters out unacceptable views. This leads to silly results like the holiday work proposal."

The governor's early appointments showed the same lack of balance: his new clemency secretary was a former assistant district attorney who had campaigned for capital punishment; the real estate commissioner was a realtor who advocated repeal of fair-housing laws; the industrial-relations director (traditionally a union member) was a management representative. But when he was asked about his appointments Reagan said, "If I appoint him, he's qualified."

In the first months the administration reacted like a fire brigade to each day's crises. When things got tough the governor used massive retaliation: he went on television. There he was free of uncertainty and dissent, and he could play the embattled chief fighting for his "Creative Society."

He was so effective on TV and the mood of California was so anti-government that the less Reagan did, the higher he stood with the voters. When the pollsters asked Californians what Reagan had done specifically to win their approval, most could not cite a single accomplishment, pointing instead to his style and public statements. When Reagan was not on television giving California the big picture he got restless. He fidgeted and tapped his fingers at meetings when there were no crises, but he quickly encountered more troubles than he had anticipated.

The administration had its first major crisis when it decided to trim the University of California's budget. Reagan asked the Board of Regents, the most prestigious laymen's body in California, to cut its request of $278 million by $82 million, more than 25 per cent of the total. Although enrollment was climbing each year, the cut would have meant a 20 per cent reduction from the *current* year's appropriation, and it would have severely strained the University's capacity to handle an expected enrollment of 90,000 and hire 530 new professors.

Meanwhile, the trustees of the California State College System proposed a budget of $213 million, an increase of about $37 million, to accommodate approximately 144,000 students on 18 campuses and to hire 700 professors. Reagan limited the state colleges to the budget for the current year. To make up some of the difference, the governor suggested that the University and the colleges spend their reserve funds and charge tuition.

When the governor tried to explain his stand he made it sound like a continuation of the campaign. At a press conference Reagan declared that "[tuition] would help get rid of undesirables. Those there to agitate and not to study might think twice before they pay tuition. They might think twice how much they want to pay to carry a picket sign." His own words supported his critics' suspicion that the governor was using the economy argument as a cover to castrate the University.

California's most influential newspaper, the Los Angeles *Times*, which endorsed Reagan, editorialized:

> The University and state colleges apparently have been singled out for such treatment because of Reagan's reaction to unrest on the UC Berkeley campus. The demonstrations were unfortunate, often deplorable, and frequently mishandled. But they also involved only a small minority of the students—plus nonstudents on one campus.
>
> The *Times* believes that the governor has badly misread his mandate from the people if he thinks they intended him to punish the entire University and state college system because of the incidents of a relatively few students. . . .

Reagan's finance director, Gordon Smith, proposed a
10 per cent reduction in state-supported research as an
alternative to an enrollment cutback. But research has
helped California agriculture in harvest techniques,
crop development and elimination of blight. The proposal was quickly dropped. Smith then suggested that
professors might teach more classes "just to help out this
one year." This suggestion also failed because first-rate
professors, eagerly sought by universities, are attracted
to campuses where they can perform research and in-
struct small classes.

Reagan proposed tuition of $250 to $280 at the University and $150 to $160 in the state colleges. But this would
have meant an increased enrollment in California's
eighty junior colleges, which are supported by property
taxes, and the governor was pledged to give relief to
property taxpayers. He also proposed that part of the
tuition be used to grant scholarships to poor students;
but this would wipe out any substantial savings to the
state, which was Reagan's pretext for requesting the
change in the first place.

The budget fight was complicated by the dismissal of
Clark Kerr at the first regents' meeting Reagan attended
as governor. Under Kerr the University had doubled its
enrollment and increased from two to nine campuses.
But the regents felt he had mishandled the demonstrations and would have fired him two years earlier if not
for Pat Brown's intercession. Although Reagan did not
engineer the dismissal, he voted for it and educators
throughout the country described the discharge as anti-
intellectual and vindictive. Kerr, who had accumulated

a welter of scars in handling the University's problems, had never been so popular before his dismissal.

Assembly Speaker Unruh, an ex-officio regent like Reagan, emerged from the meeting looking, for once, as distressed as he said he was. Unruh, who had disagreed with Kerr on many issues, had defended the University president and the regents' original budget. The speaker, who had once been considered an enemy, suddenly became a hero on campus. "Jesse Saves" buttons sprang up on students and professors, while the campus blossomed with placards declaring "Recast Reagan" and "Cut Reagan by 10 Per Cent." Before his first month in office, the new governor had been hanged in effigy on campus.

But Kerr was irrevocably gone, and the New Left shared the Far Right's joy. Mario Savio enthused: "Governor Reagan is off to an auspicious start. Good riddance to bad rubbish."

No one could deliver on Reagan's campaign promises to roll back government. But in his first months, Reagan acted as if he could: he announced massive cutbacks and back-tracked a few weeks later. Even when he failed, the voters applauded him for trying. However, fiscal reality kept darkening Reagan's vision. Nearly two-thirds of California's budget is mandated for schools, welfare and highways. The remaining one-third represents the state's operating expenses. Of this amount, approximately 40 per cent goes toward higher education, and 17 per cent for mental health. If an administration is serious about reductions, it must cut in these two sensitive areas.

On March 27, 1967, the governor announced he was cutting fifteen state mental health facilities and abolishing 3,700 positions in the Department of Mental Hygiene for a savings of $17.7 million. Reagan had consulted with Richard Krabach, finance director for Republican Governor James Rhodes in Ohio. But Ohio should have been a lesson in reverse: four years after Rhodes cut Ohio's mental-health budget by 10 per cent, he found it necessary to ask for $95 million for mental health plus a six-year building program that will cost approximately $250 million.

The administration justified the cutback on the statistical basis that California's inmate population in mental-health hospitals was down from 36,000 to 24,000 in the last eight years. But the caseload had been reduced because California had spent *more*, not less, for intensive treatment at hospitals, thus shortening the average stay of patients. In New York, Governor Rockefeller asked for an increase of $38.6 million, and 4,500 new staff positions although the state's mental-inmate population had dropped.

If the community clinics and day treatment centers were abolished, as Reagan requested, marginal patients would have to be institutionalized, and the inmate population would go up again.

"It would appear that the governor justifies his budget cuts on the basis of reduced caseloads and then applies the cuts to the very facilities that helped reduce the number of institutional patients," the Los Angeles *Times* commented. "Furthermore, he proposed that the

counties spend millions of dollars more in local funds
[to pick up the caseloads] just at the time that he pro-
poses that the state help reduce local property taxes."

The San Francisco *Chronicle* described the day-care
centers, which Reagan wanted to eliminate, as one of
"the most successful mental-health experiments in the
nation."

The Sacramento *Bee* noted that the Reagan claim of a
fiscal crisis ignored the fact that Californians' personal
income reached a record $70 billion in 1966. "But it is far
easier," the *Bee* editorialized, "to oppose progressive
and accepted governmental services by pretending
poverty, instead of opposing them on ideological
grounds, thus revealing a rather unpopular bias against
free education and other needed public services."

A legislative expert in mental hygiene explained: "The
cuts don't make sense either in terms of program or
economy. If the cuts were approved, it would place a
tremendous burden on the counties, who would have to
raise property taxes to operate day treatment centers.
And Reagan is pledged to lower property taxes."

The remaining illusions crumbled when Reagan
ended his first legislative session by signing a $5.08-
billion budget and a $933-million tax increase to finance
it. It was the largest budget in history for any state and,
to make it more palatable to his original supporters,
Reagan exercised the governor's power of line-item veto
to cut $43.5 million. Again he used token gestures to in-
sure a public relations gain but the cuts showed the
administration's direction: nearly $6 million from the
University, $3.4 million from state colleges, $2 million

from the anti-poverty program, $11.4 million from mental hygiene and nearly $12 million from salary increases for state employees.

The reductions made no real dent in California's financial problems and they failed to appease Reagan's conservative supporters, who felt the governor could have been a lot tougher if he were not thinking about the White House. By the start of his second legislative session, it was clear that Reagan had misled his most dedicated supporters into believing that he could cut spending. During the campaign, when he accused Pat Brown of not leveling with the people, he sounded convincing; but in just one year he had slipped into the same evasions and self-deceptions.

His administration extracted some solace from the claim that Reagan had reduced the *rate* of budgetary increase from 16 to 8 per cent, but it was inevitable that the budget would increase, whoever was governor. Republicans in the Legislature conceded that Reagan might have to ask for another tax increase within two years. And next time he would not be able to blame the Democrats. Eventually, Reagan will have to "level with the people" and face the consequences.

11

The Presidential Noncandidate

If Ronald Reagan decides he wants to run, he will be the Republican nominee in 1968. But I don't think he wants it.

> —Barry M. Goldwater, May 3, 1967, press conference in St. Louis

Ronald Reagan may find it easier to run for President than to seek reelection as governor in 1970. After fourteen months in office Reagan has shown little desire to confront the state problems that mount behind his wall of rhetoric. But he obviously enjoys touring the countryside in triumph as a Presidential noncandidate, and the crowds cheer him just as in the days when he toured for General Electric.

Meanwhile, his second legislative session opened on a sour note after he dragooned Republicans into a quixotic fight to unseat Assembly Speaker Jesse Unruh and Senate President Pro Tem Hugh Burns. After the

Democrats beat him down, Reagan tried to evade responsibility for the defeat by picking a fight with Jesse Unruh. "It would seem," he declared, "that it takes more than a change of tailor to change the image of Big Daddy."

It was the kind of crack (which Spencer-Roberts steered him away from in 1966) that needlessly offends. Unruh, who hates his nickname, listened grimly to a taped recording of Reagan's press conference remarks. "This isn't going to make the session any easier," he said. In fact, Unruh can make life miserable for Reagan, who wants to bring a solid legislative record into the 1968 convention.

In public-relations terms, the governor might gain a short-run benefit from a fight with Unruh. The billing has that neat Good-Bad touch so beloved in Hollywood Westerns: Ronald Reagan, White Hat, versus Jesse Unruh, Tammany Type. But Unruh has friends in both parties, and he was trading favors with them while Reagan was fighting Bad Guys on television. Meanwhile, the state suffers because its government is disrupted by warfare between the governor and the lawmakers.

But problems beyond 1968 are academic to a Presidential candidate who barely conceals his boredom with parochial topics. When reporters bog him down in a state issue, a sigh of boredom escapes. Occasionally the tedium of Sacramento is relieved by international news, and the governor happily seizes the chance to make a hawkish pronouncement. When North Korea captured the U.S. spy ship *Pueblo*, Reagan issued an ultimatum: The *Pueblo* must be returned in twenty-four hours or the United States should go in and get it. After considerable reflection, Reagan amended his foreign policy, stating that he had not meant that the Navy should tie a tow rope to the *Pueblo* and pull it out. He further hedged his original declaration by adding, "if the facts are as we are told they are." Thus the Reagan technique: a nice little headline the first day and an ambiguous backdown the next. It accomplished nothing but reminded everyone that Reagan is available for bigger tasks. Reagan has done more than hint; a shadow organization has been assembling a White House drive in his behalf.

Henry A. Salvatori has directed the governor's Presidential campaign since the inauguration. From his Los Angeles office he regularly telephones the oilmen and financiers who backed Goldwater. Meanwhile, Salvatori has kept a tight checkrein on the operation; and each move is run as a fire drill for the next step up the ladder—the Goldwater speech, the primary, the general election, the preconvention trips, the careful disclaimers of ambition.

By early 1968 Salvatori had assembled a smoothly running Presidential machine which he continues to lubricate with money and talent. After the inauguration, a thirty-two-year-old aide, Tom Reed, quit as appointments secretary and traveled around the countryside to meet party chairmen. Other workers are checking delegates in potentially hot Reagan areas in the South and Midwest. Salvatori, who is to Reagan what Joe Kennedy was to his son's chances in 1960, also hired F. Clifton

White, the 1964 convention wizard for Goldwater. White, who clung for months to the fiction that he was uncommitted, is quietly checking on delegates attached to Richard M. Nixon and whipping up Reagan fever among Young Republicans for a 1968 blitz.

Salvatori considered the original avowed candidates, Nixon and George Romney, as stand-ins for the real contenders—Reagan and Rockefeller—whom he had expected to surface in Miami Beach. Although Reagan and Rockefeller are on opposite poles, ideologically and geographically, the governors maintain an underground channel of communication. Spencer-Roberts mans the "hot line" in the West and National Committeeman George Hinman, Rockefeller's chief consultant, in the East. The two noncandidates originally shared an aura of mystery more potent than the workaday vibrations emanating from the declared candidates. Reagan's chief asset has been his image of integrity, which could vanish overnight if Californians realized for how long he has been planning to run out on his four-year contract; meanwhile, Rockefeller carries the scars of 1964 and the old conservative wounds ache when the press speculates about a Rockefeller-Reagan ticket.

In the early preprimary maneuvering, Rockefeller's supporters briefly entertained the idea of Reagan acting as a stalking horse to kill off Nixon in the primaries, thus making possible the "dream ticket" of Rockefeller-Reagan. But Reagan has never liked second billing and he has steadfastly denied any interest in the job, although Bill Roberts of Spencer-Roberts thinks Reagan might be persuaded to take number two by convention time. By the end of March, 1968, one of the most hectic months in the history of American politics, the scenario had changed completely: first Romney dropped out, then Rockefeller (who still kept himself available for a draft), then President Johnson. In five weeks the face of American politics, 1968, had changed astoundingly: it left Nixon the front-runner in the Republican party, as he had been for months, but it also meant he would be deprived of his most vulnerable target, an unpopular President saddled with a disastrous war and riots at home.

If Nixon cannot wrap up the nomination before the convention, he will face serious trouble in the form of "favorite son" candidacies set up to block a nomination on the first ballot. Once the convention goes to a second ballot, it is possible that Nixon's early support will diminish and Reagan will emerge.

Meanwhile, Nixon is saddled with a double burden of irony; now he is the scarred old warhorse. In 1952, as a thirty-nine-year-old senator with ambitions, he sabotaged California's favorite son, Earl Warren, to win the number two spot on the Eisenhower ticket. But the wheel has come full cycle for Nixon, who checks his conservative flank each time Reagan tours the country with his flashing smile and simplistic oratory. Reagan, of course, artfully dismisses his out-of-state trips as necessary fund-raising chores for the party; F. Clifton White, whose presence is not so easily explained, is acknowledged as a hired hand who will "interpret trends" for the California delegation, and Reagan continues his Presidential disavowals. After repeating his weekly disclaimer, Reagan declared his availability for a "draft" on April 26, 1967: "Sherman is the only fellow who ever made a Sherman-like statement, and I figured he played that to the hilt."

Nixon, hoping since 1964 to inherit Goldwater's following, has not been popular with conservatives since he bought peace with the GOP liberals by signing Rockefeller's 1960 "Treaty of Fifth Avenue." Besides, he has been around too long and the years of crises and compromises have dimmed his luster. Although he is a man without a political base, Nixon benefits from widespread but shallow support among delegates who recall that he has always been a regular who worked for the GOP in good years and bad. But the old campaigner in 1968 resembles a sober and stolid party steward while Reagan is the potent heartthrob who can be wooed and won. Barry Goldwater, honoring a commitment made in 1964, insists that he is pledged to Nixon but he does little to stop the speculation that his heart belongs to Reagan. The conservative theoreticians at William F. Buckley's *National Review* are nominally with Nixon but dismiss him with faint praise and light up with a messianic glow when Reagan's name is mentioned. Nixon, who has skewered many a rival, now finds himself the victim of an old ploy, that patronizing and lethal judgment, "He can't win."

In Oregon, the Reagan-for-President group is spending $300,000 to topple Nixon in the May primary. Most of the money is going into television, where Oregonians

are reminded by political spot announcements that
Nixon couldn't beat Pat Brown. The campaign has only
intensified the occasional subterranean hostility between Nixon and Reagan. As a result, Nixon's staff
leaked a story to the Los Angeles *Times* that it is "baf-
fled" by Reagan's exertions in Oregon. Meanwhile,
Reagan continued the diplomatic infighting by reminding the press that favorite-son candidates control
enough delegates to block anyone from getting the
nomination on the first ballot. The relationship between
Nixon and Reagan is subtle and convoluted; each sees
the other as a threat but also as a potential source of
support if and when the convention gets bogged down
beyond the first ballot.

In the early primaries Reagan and Rockefeller have
tried to orchestrate a tricky minuet; Rockefeller has
stayed out of the primaries because an overt move
would precipitate a conservative uprising; Reagan, who
got 11 per cent of the primary vote in Wisconsin, the first
state in which he was listed on the ballot, said he was
surprised and flattered but insisted that he is not a candidate. Nixon, who got 80 per cent in Wisconsin, is left
with the unsatisfying knowledge that he defeated an
avowed noncandidate, Reagan, and a perennial candidate, Harold Stassen. Nonetheless, Nixon will control
the largest bloc of delegates in Miami Beach, and it is
conceivable that, if he cannot make it, he could throw
his support to a dark-horse candidate to frustrate those
who deprived him of the nomination.

Each week new rumors crop up about Reagan's Presi-

dential maneuvers and, mindful of Californians' mistrust
of being used, Reagan entertains his weekly audience
with protestations of innocence. But his disavowals fail
to convince the press on the Legislative in bemused
Sacramento. When *Time* quoted Reagan as telling an
unnamed governor that "Nixon cannot win; he couldn't
even beat Pat Brown," Reagan denied it. Hearst columnist Marianne Means reported that Reagan had talked
politics with Governor Paul Johnson of Mississippi, and
Reagan contended that he had never met Johnson.
When the columnist produced a photograph of the two
governors at a Washington conference, Reagan's office
acknowledged the men had met but insisted the encoun-
ter was perfunctory. When Reagan and Nixon met in
July, 1967, at Bohemian Grove, a wooded retreat north of
San Francisco, Reagan declared, "I have a strange
hunch that 1968 won't even come up in our discussion." But Nixon later announced that he had agreed
not to tamper with Reagan's favorite-son delegation.

Reagan remains popular despite his growing credibility gap because the California voters, who have been
misled for so long, desperately want to believe in someone. And they accept Reagan because he does not
appear to be the slick politician that he really is. But the
image is wearing thin as Reagan's White House fever
rages; he is hurt not so much by his lies (he does not lie
more than most politicians) but by his holier-than-thou
attitude that he is above chicanery and by his absurd
outbursts when he is caught.

He suffered a significant loss of face in November,
1967, after columnist Drew Pearson published a report

that had circulated for weeks in the Capitol about a homosexual ring that included two men on the governor's staff. One was "probably the closest to Reagan in his entire public life," the columnist reported, and the others included an "athletic adviser" and several men prominent in California politics. Details of the story had been confirmed by Reagan's director of communications, Lyn Nofziger, who told three reporters about it in an off-the-record discussion during the 1967 governors' cruise on the SS *Independence*. The governor tried to brazen it out with a lie at his press conference. He shouted and hammered at his lectern, his face darkening with anger. "He's lying," Reagan said of the columnist. His lips compressed, eyes driving holes into the reporters, Reagan denied what virtually everyone in the room knew: Nofziger had confirmed the story. The shirt-sleeved, stubby Nofziger stood nearby, sweating with anxiety. "He's here," said Reagan, pointing to Nofziger, "and you can ask him directly. I am prepared to say that nothing like that ever happened. . . . Want to confirm it, Lyn?" Nofziger, whose face was constricted with embarrassment, muttered "confirmed" and kept his eyes averted.

The details had been known for weeks; in fact, *Newsweek* had hinted at the brewing scandal a week before Pearson's column. The columnist mistakenly contended that Reagan had harbored the two homosexual staffers for six months but Nofziger had told reporters that Reagan acted immediately after his assistants brought him proof. The evidence consisted of letters and tape recordings of a party in a cabin at Lake Tahoe. An investigation revealed that the two staffers had had homosexual inclinations since they were teen-agers. The governor asked the higher-ranking aide to meet him at his home and, without referring to the accusation or the evidence, simply told his assistant, "I think it is time for you to return to private life." The staffer understood what had happened and agreed to resign immediately; the other man was brought back from a conference in Washington and cashiered the next day. Both have since disappeared from public view and the Reagan administration went to the trouble of emphasizing that neither had any further connection with the governor's office. But the unhappy facts did not hurt Reagan as much as his decision to bluff a knowing group of reporters when he could have drawn the cloak of executive secrecy over the matter. Reagan again had succumbed to a reckless impulse and, when the noose tightened, he let his anger show. His performance was even more puzzling because, on the face of it, he had acted prudently. Confronted with the charge, he sought proof; when he got it, he demanded resignations immediately and tried to keep the matter private. But when the facts came out, he revealed a grievous inability to remain calm under pressure. Had he acted to preserve a reputation, that would have been understandable, but he could have done so without discussing it or bothering to deny it. Instead, he acted like a man obsessed with the need to preserve his image at all costs.

Another crack in the façade showed up on that same cruise aboard the SS *Independence* during which Nofziger confirmed the homosexual story. During the cruise, Reagan displayed a copy of a White House cable. It had been sent by Presidential Assistant Marvin Watson to Price Daniel, former governor of Texas, and urged Daniel to question Republican Governors Rhodes of Ohio and Chafee of Rhode Island about their stand on the resolution. The cable noted that the governors in the past had supported the President's policy. Reagan used the confidential wire to embarrass the President (who was contending that he was not pressuring any of the governors). At first it seemed to be a brilliant public-relations move by Reagan which resulted in the defeat of the White House resolution. But it also got the governor involved in an undignified argument over how he got possession of the wire. The governor insisted that it was accidentally handed him by a ship's employee (whom he could not identify), but others on board contended that Reagan's ubiquitous assistant, Nofziger, had been handing out copies. Nofziger, smiling bravely throughout the furore, denied that he had bribed a ship's radioman to get a copy, but the incident left a sour impression on Reagan's fellow passengers, who felt that if he had received the wire by mistake he was honor bound to return it immediately without revealing its contents.

Since the Drew Pearson column Nofziger has been in disfavor with the governor, who denies weekly reports that Nofziger is leaving. Nofziger is a shrewd former Washington columnist for the Copley Newspapers, and he has won his share of power struggles within the administration. He is a tough and abrasive man who does not hesitate to call reporters into his office and reprimand them for stories he considers biased. Although Mrs. Reagan is distressed by his rumpled paunch and brusque manner, the governor retains him because Nofziger is a talented operator who draws off criticism that otherwise would be directed at the governor.

But the inside ferment is unknown outside Sacramento; when Reagan moves in public, he looks like a winner. At a breakfast in Omaha he brought 500 Nebraska Republicans to their feet by declaring, "I think we should win that war as quickly as possible. . . . Ho Chi Minh should be sitting on an apple crate asking for help." At the Western governors' conference in West Yellowstone, Montana, he wore beige ranch denims with "Governor Ronald Reagan" stitched on the jacket and the photographers flocked around him. He galvanized a Republican fund-raising dinner that had been left gasping for air after George Romney's woolly platitudes. When Reagan posed for pictures with the other candidates, they looked shopworn by comparison.

He also benefits from the notion, prevalent among some intellectuals, that a right-of-center politician cannot hold his own in debate. But he deflated another magnetic personality, Robert F. Kennedy, on CBS' *Town Meeting of the World.* While Kennedy anguished through questions about the war from hostile European students, the tanned and relaxed governor talked easily and precisely without a hint of uncertainty or hostility. He had prepared for the telecast by studying a twelve-page memorandum and the governor was so thoroughly briefed by air time that he could correct the statistics of one of his questioners. Actually, Reagan did not want to appear at first, but when he heard the senator from New York was the guest, he jumped at the chance. By the end of the show Kennedy looked as if he had stumbled into a minefield. The senator often was found looking into the wrong lens, while Reagan kept his gaze riveted on the right camera. Kennedy tried to recover with an upbeat quote that he had used before, but Reagan came right back with one of *his* set pieces about man reaching for the stars, and Kennedy gulped in restrained agony. At Yale University the governor disarmed hostile questioners with good-humored replies. The first question at the start of his three-day visit was one he anticipated: should homosexuals be permitted in government? Reagan reflected for a moment: "Well . . . maybe in the Department of Parks and Recreation." Having defused his tormentors' prime weapon, the governor snuffed out lingering pockets of resistance with leftover anecdotes and statistics from his campaign, and the students had to concede that he was persuasive if not totally convincing.

Reagan's out-of-state triumphs have helped him stifle dissatisfaction within his own party at home; few politicians want to risk an open break with a favorite son who can stir mob scenes like Kennedy's 1960 crowds. Because his popularity remains high, Reagan can make deals that ordinarily would cause fratricide within the GOP. For instance, he made peace with Senator Thomas Kuchel, who refused to endorse him or Murphy. The old professional magicians, Spencer and Roberts, worked out the détente. Reagan, who thinks Kuchel is excessive in his concern with the Right, agreed to remain neutral in the 1968 U.S. Senate primary; Kuchel faces opposition from a popular and doctrinaire conservative, Dr. Max Rafferty, state superintendent of public instruction. Kuchel, who detests the Right for smearing him as a traitor and a homosexual, agreed to let Reagan lead without hindrance a favorite-son delegation, and both men promised to cooperate on federal-state problems. The two men, who lead factions violently opposed to each other, posed for photographs with the stiff-faced formality usually reserved for diplomats of unfriendly nations.

Reagan's most dedicated supporters, the conservatives, were incensed by the Kuchel agreement. Dr. Rafferty discovered that his fund-raising sources had dried up after a talk with Henry Salvatori. When Salvatori talks, politicians listen, and the industrialist told Rafferty that he was doing a good job where he was and that he did not want a costly primary fight that could wreck Reagan's dream of leading a united delegation. Conservatives who had struggled for Reagan when his candidacy was a joke to everyone else realized that they could not count on help from operators like Salvatori, and Rafferty had to rely heavily on contributions from out of state.

"Even conservative businessmen had to accept the logic of a deal with Kuchel," reasoned a prime financial backer for Kuchel. "As a big state with heavy industry, California needs good relations with the federal government. Businessmen realize this means millions to the state in defense contracts, shipbuilding, highways and research grants and they recognize that Kuchel knows his way around the Establishment after fourteen years in Washington. This is no time to send a hard right-winger to represent California, especially when we are fighting Texas and New York for that federal dollar. California now has a guy who can *deliver,* and it doesn't make sense to take a chance on an unknown. A new governor like Reagan needs all the help he can get in Washington and his willingness to make a deal with Tommy shows that he really is serious about the Presidency. Reagan knows his chances ride on how he does in California."

Once again California conservatives are beginning to feel they have been used, but they have nowhere to go; Reagan no longer needs them, they need him. For six years they had dreamed of an assault on Kuchel and they assumed that a Reagan victory would mean just that. But they discovered by the end of the first legislative session that Reagan was, at heart, "another politician." The Right is not yet in full rebellion in California, but there are mutterings from conservative volunteer leaders who want an open GOP primary. The only avowed Bircher in the Legislature, State Senator John Schmitz, criticizes Reagan for not making heavier cuts in the budget. But criticism from a Bircher meshes beautifully with the White House plans of a governor who wants to appeal to moderates, and there are skeptics who wonder if Schmitz is playing a double game.

Meanwhile, the governor's problems intensify as he tries to straddle the inevitable contradictions that emanate from California politics. He dilutes his conservatism to pick up moderates, while he reassures conservatives that he still is one of them. It is an excruciatingly delicate maneuver, and Pat Brown, who tried to appeal to both wings of his party, eventually fell in the chasm between them. So far Reagan has avoided disaster by clinging to conservative rhetoric while easing moderates into important positions. He appointed former State GOP Chairman Caspar Weinberger to succeed Gordon Smith as director of finance. Weinberger, a moderate who was once part of Nixon's team, originally was turned down by Reagan's selection committee because he was considered too liberal and too close to Nixon. But after Smith antagonized the Legislature, Reagan yielded him up as the price for legislative harmony. And inch by inch, the doctrinaire assumptions of an erstwhile right-wing ideologue are battered down by political necessity.

To reassure conservatives, Reagan makes bold noises about budgeteering forays, but the sum of his reductions remains less than a fraction of 1 per cent of the state budget. And all but the most intransigent conservatives realize that Reagan cannot deliver (nor could any other governor) on his promise to substantially diminish state spending. He delays the inevitable disillusionment by continuing to attack social-welfare programs. This tactic is politically safe because his middle-class constituency wants relief from these burdens. "In some ways," Jesse Unruh commented, "the governor has the best of both worlds. He establishes his image as a great economizer and then he backs down after the uproar and everybody breathes a sigh of relief and says, 'He's not such a bad guy after all.' "

"I was quite a bleeding-heart liberal," Reagan explains in denying that he lacks compassion for others. "I think I have some understanding of how they think and how I thought, and the criticism that I have and many of my friends—and we discuss this good-naturedly because they still are my friends—but there's been a tendency with regard to social legislation, that when anyone like myself is opposed to some proposed social legislation, the other side never will meet you on the legitimate argument as to whether that particular legislation is the best way to solve the problem. They only want to argue by charging that you are against the humanitarian goals. Now, I said I am wholeheartedly in support of the humanitarian goals of practically all of the social legislation we have ever had. I am violently opposed to some of the methods we have chosen because they have not brought the good they were supposed to bring. I don't think there is any real good to humanity or compassion in adopting some kind of welfare that perpetuates poverty and puts people for three and four generations of their family onto the public dole instead of getting them off the public dole and out as self-sustaining citizens, and this charge is going to continue to be made. I know, and the only hope that I can have now in this position is to hope that we will try our way and maybe they will see as the end result that we did some good and that we did have compassion after all."

Reagan's denial is almost airtight: he agrees with

humanitarian goals but he opposes the bureaucratic inefficiency that infests so many programs. But Reagan is careful not to attack bureaucratic incompetence in programs that are popular with his middle-class constituents. If he had principled objections to the concept of government intercession he could find excesses in the politically safe programs, like old-age pensions and unemployment insurance, but instead he views with alarm those programs designed to assist the weakest and most vulnerable elements in society. Even in his liberal days Reagan showed little concern for the poor. When he was making $3,500 a week in Hollywood he inveighed against the injustice of the graduated income tax, not the plight of families who made less than $3,500 a year.

It is true that Reagan, like most Americans, worked hard to gain a measure of the world's abundance, but he usually had someone to help him. Now he refuses to recognize that others not so generously endowed in personality and appearance have no one to intercede for them. He has been so busy reaching for the next rung that he does not relate to those on the bottom rung as human beings born with the same potential but spiritually devastated from infancy. It is not a question of Reagan turning his back on the dispossessed; he simply does not *see* them. In the old days, before Spencer-Roberts smoothed out his rough edges, he referred to pensioners as a "faceless mass waiting for hand-outs." To Reagan, "they" will always be a faceless mass, in all their human weakness and error, because they threaten his vision of a clean and well-ordered society. He dismisses arguments for these casualties of the American Dream as the special pleading of "bleeding hearts."

Despite his patronizing self-characterization, Reagan was never really a bleeding heart or a "nearly hopeless hemophilic liberal." His supposed liberalism was not based on broad humanist concerns but on fears about his own economic position.

Although there is nothing in his private or public life to indicate that he ever was motivated by selfless idealism, Reagan has the ability to convince others (and possibly himself) that he was and is. The woods are full of pragmatic and acquisitive men, but it takes a superb politician to appear otherwise and, having come from an industry that excels in artifice, it is not surprising that Reagan succeeded in a calling that requires similar talents.

He succeeds because of the public's adoration of glamorous figures; he did not create that demand for political sex appeal, which has been fed by television and public relations, but he is a logical consequence of it, and there are other Reagans to take his place when his fans become disenchanted. The opposition, which complains about the slick marketing techniques in selling Reagan, uses the same tools but not as skillfully.

There is a faint air of nostalgia in Ronald Reagan's evocations of a "Creative Society" and all the other set phrases about the long climb from the swamp to the stars. Perhaps it is an unconscious mirror image of John F. Kennedy's New Frontier and the Right's version of Kennedy's summons to get the country moving again.

When Reagan talks about rolling back government at home and making America an armed colossus abroad, it is reminiscent of the missile-gap-that-did-not-exist in 1960. Kennedy was an authentic young man, a war hero, a reflective man with the gift (and curse) of self-mockery; Reagan is a middle-aged man who affects the style of youth, an expert in imagery who cannot abide anyone who tries to look beyond the barrier he has erected. But in a time of uncertainty and frustration he projects a promise of new directions as Kennedy did in 1960. After another summer of riots America may become weary and disenchanted with a government that keeps moving toward an ill-defined and seemingly unattainable goal, a vision of which the current President has difficulty in articulating. Then the voters might look for a man who excels at communicating.

They may look to California and see what Reagan has wrought with his vision. They will see what happens when the voters get tired of government and its works. It is a measure of Reagan's skill that he exploited their grievances so superbly as to prevent the voters from really considering the alternative. California made it clear in 1966 that it wanted something different; it is a supreme irony that, despite millions spent and enormous energies consumed, California will only get more of the same.

Index

JOSEPH LEWIS served as a *Time* magazine correspondent in the Los Angeles area
from 1963 until the fall of 1967. He began his
coverage of the California political scene in
1959 with the Associated Press. Earlier, he had
been with the Seattle and Phoenix bureaus of
the AP.

Mr. Lewis, now a freelance writer, has been
a contributor to several magazines. He
attended UCLA and is a veteran of the
Korean War. A Californian by adoption,
he lives with his wife and children in Man-
hattan Beach.